Huntingdon Area
Middle School Library
Huntingdon, Pa.

# MOTORCYCLING

# MOTORCYCLING
## and the new enthusiast

written by Peter H. Salinger / designed by Joseph A. Phelan

**GROSSET & DUNLAP**
Publishers  New York

12668

Library of Congress Catalog Card Number: 73-825
ISBN: 0-448-11500-4 (Trade Edition)
ISBN: 0-448-03931-1 (Library Edition)

Copyright ©1973, by Peter H. Salinger and Joseph A. Phelan.
All rights reserved under International and Pan-American
 Copyright Conventions.
Printed in the United States of America.
Published simultaneously in Canada.

## To Bobbie:
## for her love, patience,
## and understanding.

*Additional photography by the author, Thaxton & Levine (ppgs. 78-79,87 Kawasaki ,91), Bruce Kirstein (pg. 89-Triumph Matisse), Leighton Smith (pg.81).*

*Many thanks for help and encouragement to: John Yaw, AMA News; Peter Suto, MIC; Jack & Jim Nash, Nash Brothers New Haven; Oscar Libby, Libby's Sales & Service; Stewart Bronstien, Cape Cod Motor Sport Center; Richard Kahn, Butler & Smith New Jersey; Tom Sargent and Phil Schilling, Cycle Magazine; Howard Kokubun, American Honda; Laura Hochenedel, Husqvarna Motorcorp East; unsigned people at Triumph East, Pabatco and Harley Davidson; Jake Engle, Cunningham & Walsh; Scott Brelsford; Yvon DuHamel; & Gary Nixon.*

# CONTENTS

| | |
|---|---|
| Introduction | 7 |
| What's it all about? | 11 |
| Mighty Mites | 22 |
| Why it works | 28 |
| Nuts, bolts, screws, hammers, pliers, and fixes | 38 |
| This is my left hand this is my right hand, and that's a motorcycle | 54 |
| Making sure the bike you buy is the bike you want | 63 |
| The folks who care | 70 |
| Good Guys/Bad Guys | 74 |
| There's only one number—No. 1 | 78 |
| Glossary | 92 |
| Address Book | 95 |

# WHAT'S IT ALL ABOUT?

What motivates a motorcyclist? What makes him ride? Why does he prefer one kind of bike over another—or one kind of road? There are probably as many answers to those questions as there are motorcyclists to answer them. It is a very personal thing, this sport of cycling, and because no two people are exactly alike, no two people ride alike or for the same reasons.

To some, the ultimate ride may be along a two-lane blacktop road as dawn begins to overcome the chill of the early hours. Passing from shady pockets of cold into patches where the sun has already set the flavor of the day. Being with the bike, sensing the changes in the road.

Others may yearn for a chance to leave the road for the solitude of a wooded trail. The best ride may be through a quiet forest at practically a walking speed, taking time to see things a little differently each time, becoming part of the surroundings. That rider may stop if a place —perhaps a stream or the crest of a hill—looks inviting. The quiet and the chance to be alone to collect his thoughts may be the very reason that he rides.

To others, still, it could be a love of traveling—setting off on a trip by oneself, watching the country change faces as the miles roll by. The cyclist may ride three or four hundred miles a day before fatigue and the night force him to find a campsite or a bed.

To some, companionship is an important consideration. Having someone to share the fun of riding might be half the fun.

If it begins to seem as though motorcyclists are just like anybody else, so be it. Plenty of people like the woods and camping, and most like a quiet country road, but there is a difference, and it's important to recognize it and try to understand it from the beginning. Cyclists are cyclists by choice. There is something in them that binds them together, regardless of where they ride, why they ride, or what kind of bike they choose to do it on. Something makes them choose to ride a motorcycle. The best way to describe that thing is to say that it is a feeling, an urge to do things a particular way. Lots of factors are involved. Certainly freedom is part of it. Freedom, not in the sense that a cyclist can do anything he wants to do, since he must operate under the same rules as anybody else. Rather, it's a freedom of his movement and of his vision, of his hearing, and his sense of smell, even his imagination. The link between a rider and a bike is much more complete and much more immediate than between a driver and a car. A motorcyclist uses both hands and both feet to operate more controls, more often, than a car driver. A motorcyclist uses his body to lean in and out of turns. He is closer to the bike, and therefore closer to the road. When he stops, he can put his feet down and touch the road. He has the freedom to see his wheels meet pavement. He's free to hear the mechanical noises of the engine, free to feel the wind against him and free to smell things around him. The smells of dry leaves, cut grass, of towns and cities, take on new meanings. He becomes aware of his surroundings. That's the freedom and that's one reason a person might choose to ride.

Another is control. That he can regulate the exact direction, the exact speed of the bike, and change either with a great degree of accuracy is important to the cyclist. Being a skillful rider means a lot to him. When he rides, he thinks about how he is riding, about how he is controlling the bike. Whether or not he thinks about it all the time is not what's important. The point is that he does think about it. How he changes gears or leans into a turn is meaningful to him. That he is in control of the smallest thing is part of why he rides.

Still, there are different moods to riding, and there are different kinds of bikes. Some are more at home on turnpikes or expressways. Some blend perfectly with the ruggedness of the woods, and others combine a little bit of both.

If a rider is very fortunate, he can afford to own and maintain a different bike for any mood he might fall into, but this situation is a rare one. For the most part, you must decide what kind of riding you're most fond of, and find a bike that fits your needs. Motorcycle manufacturers recognize this, and some solve the problems by providing a wide range of bikes, covering all the bases from "strictly for the street" to full racers. Other manufacturers concentrate on one type of cycle, feeling that they can produce a better bike by limiting their efforts to pleasing one type of rider. As examples, Honda and Yamaha produce almost every kind of bike you could ever want. Husqvarna is known as a maker of rugged off-road bikes, while the smooth, silent BMW is a tradition on the open road.

Hopefully, these approaches work well for the manufacturers, since they definitely work for the cyclist. The motorcycle buyer is presented with as wide a field to choose from as he could want. This, however, can sometimes be a problem to a new rider. He may find himself with too many choices. There are guidelines for picking the bike that's right for you in the chapter on buying a bike.

The type of riding that a bike will be used for determines how the bike is designed. For the sake of simplifying things in the beginning, let's say that here are two basic areas of use—bikes for road use, and bikes for off-road use.

There are things built into a woods machine that help in the woods, but might well be a hindrance on the highway. It is also true that a bike intended for use on the road might be a great disadvantage off the road. The most obvious differences between a road bike and an off-road bike are things like overall size, tires, handlebars, and the location of exhaust pipes.

Tires for the dirt have large knobs with big spaces in between. This is so the tire can get a good grip in loose dirt or mud. Not surprisingly, these tires are called "knobbies." On a paved road, knobbies vibrate quite a bit, and they tend to wobble on fast corners. Road tires are more like passenger-car tires in appearance, with an even tread pattern. They don't grip well in dirt, and are more likely to slide sideways or skid in a dirt turn.

*One good way to spend a Sunday afternoon. This Suzuki 250 handles two-up riding and offers reasonable comfort and performance. Long trips, or a need to carry baggage for two might require a bigger bike. Above (left to right): a Suzuki TC-125J, Yamaha RD-250, and Honda 250.*

Another concept of the perfect afternoon is this gathering of off-road enthusiasts. Good examples of protective clothing can be noted. Gloves, leathers, boots and headgear add safety to the fun. Above (left to right): a BSA Lightning 650, Mark's Suzuki, and a Honda 750 four, with windshield and partial fairing—a neat set-up for touring.

There are plenty of both large and small road bikes but, for the most part, woods bikes are small. The reasons for this are simple to understand. A bigger bike has a tough time getting through the tight spaces an off-road rider can come across. Weight is another consideration. Generally, heavy bikes are less agile than their lightweight counterparts, and can be harder to control on slippery surfaces. No less important is the fact that the heavier the bike is, the harder it would be to push back to the road in the event of a breakdown.

Off-road bikes have wider, flatter handlebars. This is to give the rider more leverage, which helps him keep the front wheel pointed in the right direction on rough ground. The style of handlebars a rider chooses, however, is largely a matter of personal preference. The off-road rider might prefer narrow bars so he can get in and out of tight places without snagging brush or low branches. In any case, handlebars are not that expensive and are easily changed.

The exhaust system on a road bike is placed low and out of the way. That way there is little chance of a rider burning his leg or his pants. On a woods bike, though, low-mounted pipes might snag on rocks or logs and be damaged, so the exhaust system is kept as high and out of the way as possible. Most people who ride off the road will be (and should be) wearing protective clothing, so the risk of burns from a hot pipe is minimized. Also, it's a simple matter to mount a shield on the pipe if there is a place where the rider's leg comes too close.

There are other, less obvious differences between on- and off-road bikes. Things like gear ratios, springs, and shock absorbers are tailored to suit the type of riding that the bike is intended for.

You can see that there are many things that must be considered when a bike is built. There is a third classification of motorcycles.

Because many riders enjoy both on-road and off-road riding, several motorcycle manufacturers include bikes in their model lines that are able to take the rider to and from the woods, as well as in and out of it. This is great for people who like a little bit of all kinds of riding, and who can't afford to own (or don't want to own) two bikes. There are some disadvantages to this type of bike, though most owners of double-duty motorcycles would not consider them so. Perhaps a better word might be "compromises."

Because dirt is slipperier than pavement, one such area of compromise might be found in the braking system. If a wheel is skidding, it is, for non-racing purposes, out of control. Manufacturers of bikes for on/off road use design brake systems that will be safe in both places, but the brakes must be gentle enough to work properly in dirt. This applies a little more to the front wheel, because when the bike is stopping, its weight (and the rider's) is transferred forward, and the front wheel does most of the braking. Use that front brake. It's there for a good reason. An even application of both brakes is what you're after. Do it that way, and you'll stop as quickly and as safely as possible.

Another area of compromise could be lighting. In off-road riding, anything that projects from the bike, such as a turn signal light, is too easily torn off by brush or branches, and usually the first things to break in the event of a fall. Some people that ride the woods remove these lights and leave them home. It certainly keeps them from getting broken, but it means that the rider must give hand signals. To do that, he has to take one hand off the handlebars, which is something that should be done as little as possible. Motorcycles have only recently become equipped with directional lights as standard equipment, but anybody who owns a bike that has them will be quick to praise their convenience as well as the added safety they provide.

The headlight and taillight of a bike that is intended for on-off road use may be smaller then those found on "strictly" road bikes. This is partly to save weight (the heavier the bike, the harder to push), and partly to keep the lights from sticking out where they might be broken. It is up to the rider to compensate for any shortcomings in his lighting system by riding within its limits. Not that many off-road riders stay in the woods after sunset, but they do have to get home, and it's usually dark then. On the road, the larger and brighter your lights are, the better. You must see as far ahead as possible, and you must make sure that the other guy has every opportunity to see you.

Tires can be compromised as well. Universal tires, sometimes called trials tires, fall in between road tires and knobbies. The tread pattern is blocked, and looks like a waffle-iron griddle. In dirt, it provides better traction than a road tire, and on the road it's smoother and safer than a knobby.

Don't be talked out of owning a dual-purpose bike by the things I've called compromises. Any sacrifices you may have to make may seem a small price to pay when you realize that you can turn off the road and investigate a trail that looks inviting, with the knowledge that the bike is just as happy about it as you are.

On the road . . . off the road . . . big bikes . . . little bikes. Great. But we still don't know what's it's really like to ride. So, let's take a ride. For me, approaching my bike is kind of a thrill in itself. It's like meeting an old friend. I know the bike, and I've cured most of its ills. I've inflicted some, too, but the bike is very forgiving. It's not new, and that makes it an even better friend, since we've seen and done a lot together.

What happens next is so much a ritual for both of us that I don't think it could happen any other way. The helmet goes on, the bike gets unlocked, the stand comes up, find neutral, and it's a short roll to the street. The bike is quiet enough, but there is no point in running it near the houses if I don't have to.

Take a look at things. The oil level is fine, and there's enough gas for awhile, but I make a mental note not to get too far before I stop for fuel. I usually get about forty miles to a gallon of gas. Pull in the clutch and run the kick starter through a couple of times to take the cobwebs out of the clutch plates. Turn on the fuel tap. Turn on the key, and prime one carburetor. Nudge the starter till I find a compression stroke and bring it back to the top. The first kick brings out a friendly burbling sound that's a little rough for a second or two. Then it settles into a loping idle.

There are some things that my bike will allow me to do, and some that it won't. Starting off without a minute or so of warm-up is one of the latter. So, we sit. I've gotten used to this, and I enjoy it. I use the time to get myself ready to ride and go through a little mental conditioning. I'm a big guy, but there are times when I'm sure that I'm invisible. Why else would all those cars come so close to me on the road? I use the warm-up time to remember things like that.

With the mandatory waiting period completed, the clutch comes in, first gear is found, traffic is checked, the throttle opens a little as the clutch comes out, and the bike and I grow closer to being one and the same. Third gear brings a stop sign and the main road.

A right heads us north. Rolling up through the gears, the bike pulls steadily, and we meet the speed limit before either one of us is ready to give up the feeling of acceleration. I'm the one in charge of things like that. The bike knows that it can stop quickly from higher speeds, but it never got a ticket. I have.

The route we're on leads through a small town and then into the mountains. The road is fairly flat for the first two miles and there's little need to change gears. No hills, no turns to slow for. That will change after town as the road starts to wind upward. It's a favorite road, and we've ridden it often.

The gas station is off to the left. Ninety cents fill the tank. I'm never sad about that. The guy working the pumps wants to know how fast the bike will go. I don't know. The advertisement says 120, but I don't think I'll ever try to prove it. His reaction gives me the impression that those are not the words he wanted. After town, the road starts its stuff.

Graceful sweeping turns and quick little switchbacks. The bike and I do things we've done together many times. I watch the road, brakes slow us, gears change, the throttle draws us on, and the bike goes where I'm watching.

It wasn't always this smooth. In the beginning everything was strange and nothing worked right at all. We went through great crunching gear changes, and all too often I asked the bike to do things it never would have considered in its wildest dreams. But now it's good. There's a feeling that we are the ones standing still while the road and the land move by us. It bends, and it flattens out for a bit, and then it bends again.

The things that pass tell us where we are, how far we've gone. Leaning left, leaning right, the road winds and begins to drop back down. It's a different feeling now. A combination of sadness that the ride is half over, and a new excitement as gravity tightens up the turns. Now I think about the bike, about adjusting brakes, about not missing shifts, about the tires, and if there's sand on the next corner.

All the while the bike is working, cresting little ridges, filling in the places where the road drops out from under us, pulling corners in toward us while I watch the road, and all too soon we're down. The land flattens under us. We breathe again. It seems like it's the first breath we've taken in quite some time. At least, it's the first we've paid attention to.

Back to town, and through it, I have to force myself to keep my thoughts from staying on the mountain. Later there will be time to think about the ride. Now there's traffic and traffic signals and getting home.

In the driveway the bike gives off familiar pleasant smells as it cools, and I take off my helmet and sit on the grass for a minute, and notice, maybe for the first time, that the distance from the foot peg to the brake is the same size as my foot. Not an astounding thing, but it's the first time I haven't taken it for granted.

I check the bike pretty thoroughly when I put it away, as much from an unwillingness to leave as for anything else. But there will be other rides, and the memory of this one.

That's one of the great things about riding. The memories stay with you. When riders get together, the memories become stories, and the stories get bigger and better each time they're told. Riders do tend to group together, usually by the type of riding they mutually enjoy, so it's not surprising that clubs get formed. The formality of the clubs varies. Many are complete with elected officers, regular meetings, and planned events, while others are so loose that they're more like just the same bunch of people getting together when they feel like it.

Different people, different bikes, different reasons to ride, yes. But still, there are things all riders share—the sense of adventure, the element of risk. You can be rained on. You can be made colder than you ever thought was possible. You can fall. Those are some of the risks. You take every possible precaution to prevent things like that from happening, and preparation becomes part of the adventure. Growing sure of yourself and learning how to meet the challenges your roads offer is part of the adventure. The bike itself is an adventure.

These are some of the reasons people ride, and the fact that some prefer the open road while others like the woods or a dirt trail, or the desert, is not that important. That they choose to ride at all is reason enough to believe that they are looking for more out of going from place to place than just the satisfaction of getting there. And really, isn't that what living is supposed to be about?

There is no reason that you should have to think about the reasons you ride. There isn't any real reason why you should do anything more than enjoy yourself and your bike. But if you ride, I guarantee there will be times when you'll wonder why you ride, and you'll need to find an answer.

Some of the parts, of some of the bikes,
that make up the world of motorcycling.

# MIGHTY MITES

There are mini bikes because there are mini people. Little guys (and girls) want to ride, and there's no reason why they shouldn't. It began in a basement. A sympathetic father or older brother welded a bunch of pipe into something that resembled a frame, tied on wheels, ripped off the lawn mower motor, jammed it in the "bike," and off went the next best thing to a weekend away from home.

It wasn't long before a few enterprising individuals realized that they could do very well for themselves by turning out these backyard super-bikes in quantity and selling them to the fathers and older brothers who had managed nothing more than the destruction of an expensive piece of lawn-care equipment.

And so, the "kit" was born. It was now possible to buy all the pieces needed to build a mini, and the result was generally better, both in terms of design and family unity. Mini bikes were now, at least, somewhat more likely to make it through an afternoon without needing an overhaul, though they were still far from sophisticated.

For awhile, the sport of mini-biking was satisfied with itself. There were few improvements, and fewer outright changes. One-speed drive was the rule, as was the special "no" suspension system. The only problem was that the kids riding them got better.

The result was the mini cycle. I'm not sure who was first, and it really doesn't matter. What was important was that a major motorcycle manufacturer had seen a need—O.K., a market— and filled it. All of a sudden there were miniature motorcycles, complete in every detail, and scaled to fit four-footers. It was a good thing in a lot of ways. Initially, it was good for kids. It gave them a bike that they could work with, and one that was a bit more realistic. They wouldn't have to relearn or "unlearn" when they got big. There was a great deal of difference between the "new" bikes, and what had come before. They had transmissions, and big wheels. They had decent brakes.

These improvements meant that the minis handled like big bikes, and the dividend was that the transition to full-size was much easier and much, much safer. Additionally, because the new minis were being offered by established companies, previously unheard-of things like warranties, service, and parts availability now were part of the deal. Benefit number two.

Possibly the most important thing to come out of the arrival of mini cycles was the change of attitude that was evidenced by their riders. The kids began to care about their riding. Skill and showmanship had always been important goals, but now maturity was equally sought. Suddenly they were riding motorcycles. Small ones, to be sure, but motorcycles, nonetheless. In fact, they didn't seem small at all. They seemed, and were, just right. Responsibility was theirs, and judgment followed.

That's about where the mini bike/cycle is today. The bikes suit the riders, and the riders suit the sport. They, the riders, are continuing to develop the skills and the wisdom that will make them better adult riders.

If you're going to buy a mini, spend just as much time deciding which one to buy as you would if you were buying a full-size bike. There can be great differences from bike to bike. Some are faster than flypaper, others are slower than snails. Decide what you want. Ride them. Be honest with yourself.

Almost everything else in this book works for minis as much as big bikes. The chart that gives you "what's available" includes minis, but there's one thing that isn't mentioned elsewhere, because it pertains only to minis. Don't ride them on the road, even if they have lights, are legal, and the manufacturer says you can. They can't keep up with, get out of the way of, or be seen by, traffic. In short, they are not safe in highway situations. Anyway, why go on the road when the dirt is more fun?

*Father and son Yamahas (left). A Mini-Enduro and a 750. (top) From front to back: a Honda Mini-Trail, Suzuki Trailhopper, Honda Trail 70 and SL70, a Ford van, and a building. The Suzuki fits easily in a van or station wagon (middle). Even though it and the Yamaha mini (above) have lights, they don't belong on the road.*

# WHAT'S AVAILABLE

| Manufacturer Model | Engine Size c.c.'s | Weight lbs. | Intended Use |
|---|---|---|---|
| **Atex** | | | |
| ATX 50 | 50 | 145 | mini |
| **Benelli** | | | |
| Tornado | 650 | 463 | road |
| Supersport | 250 | 231 | road |
| Phantom | 250 | 316 | road |
| Volcano | 180 | 145 | mini |
| Enduro | 175 | 205 | dual |
| Panther | 125 | 210 | mini |
| Banchee | 90 | 155 | mini |
| Mini Enduro | 65 | 98 | mini |
| **BMW** | | | |
| R75/5 | 750 | 421 | road |
| R60/5 | 600 | 421 | road |
| R50/5 | 500 | 410 | road |
| **Bronco** | | | |
| Apache | 100 | 165 | mini |
| **BSA** | | | |
| Thunderbolt | 850 | 380 | road |
| Rocket | 750 | 455 | road |
| Lightning | 650 | 383 | road |
| Gold Star SS | 500 | 310 | road |
| Victor Trail | 500 | 298 | dual |
| Victor MX | 500 | 260 | comp |
| **Bultaco** | | | |
| Sherpa T | 350 | 213 | comp |
| Alpina | 350 | 216 | dual |
| Pursang | 350 | 225 | comp |
| Sherpa T | 250 | 209 | comp |
| Alpina | 250 | 213 | comp |
| Pursang | 250 | 220 | comp |
| Matador | 250 | 263 | dual |
| Pursang | 175 | 209 | comp |
| Alpina | 175 | 213 | dual |
| Pursang | 125 | 209 | comp |
| Alpina | 125 | 213 | dual |
| **Chapperal** | | | |
| T-100 | 100 | 140 | mini |
| ST-80 | 80 | 150 | mini |
| **CZ** | | | |
| 400MX | 400 | 234 | comp |
| 250MX | 250 | 227 | comp |
| 250 Enduro | 250 | 262 | dual |
| 175 Street-Trail | 175 | 245 | dual |
| 125MX | 125 | 209 | comp |
| **Ducati** | | | |
| 750 | 750 | 400 | road |
| RT 450 | 450 | 267 | comp |
| 350 Desmo | 350 | 252 | road |
| 250 Desmo | 250 | 249 | road |

| Manufacturer Model | Engine Size c.c.'s | Weight lbs. | Intended Use |
|---|---|---|---|
| **Harley Davidson** | | | |
| FLH-1200 | 1200 | 722 | road |
| FX-1200 | 1200 | 543 | road |
| XLCH-1000 | 1000 | 474 | road |
| XL-1000 | 1000 | 527 | road |
| SS-350 | 350 | 355 | road |
| SX-350 | 350 | 355 | dual |
| TX-125 | 125 | 232 | dual |
| SR-100 | 100 | 228 | dual |
| Z-90 | 90 | 183 | road |
| X-90 | 90 | 158 | mini |
| **Hodaka** | | | |
| 125 Wombat | 125 | 208 | dual |
| Ace 100-B | 100 | 188 | dual |
| Ace 100-MX | 100 | 173 | comp |
| **Honda** | | | |
| CB 750 four | 750 | 480 | road |
| CB 500 four | 500 | 403 | road |
| CB 450 | 450 | 400 | road |
| CL 450 | 450 | 395 | road |
| CL 350 | 350 | 350 | road |
| CB 350 | 350 | 350 | road |
| CB 350 four | 350 | 373 | road |
| SL 350 | 350 | 309 | dual |
| XL 250 | 250 | 278 | dual |
| CR 250M | 250 | 209 | comp |
| CB 175 | 175 | 284 | road |
| CL 175 | 175 | 284 | road |
| SL 175 | 175 | 249 | dual |
| CB 125S | 125 | 254 | road |
| CL 125S | 125 | 211 | road |
| SL 125 | 125 | 209 | dual |
| CB 100 | 100 | 195 | road |
| CL 100 | 100 | 195 | road |
| SL 100 | 100 | 198 | dual |
| ST 90 | 90 | 190 | mini |
| XR 75 | 75 | 141 | mini |
| CL 70 | 70 | 174 | road |
| SL 70 | 70 | 143 | dual |
| CT 70 | 70 | 154 | mini |
| Z 50 | 50 | 118 | mini |
| QA 50 | 50 | 86 | mini |
| **Husqvarna** | | | |
| 450 Desert Master | 456 | 240 | comp |
| 450 Cross Country | 456 | 240 | comp |
| 400 SC | 396 | 226 | comp |
| 360 Road & Trail | 358 | 255 | dual |
| 250 Road & Trail | 246 | 250 | dual |
| 250 Moto Cross | 246 | 220 | comp |
| 250 Cross Country | 246 | 220 | comp |
| 125 WR | 124 | 198 | comp |
| 125 CR | 125 | 198 | comp |

| Manufacturer Model | Engine Size c.c.'s | Weight lbs. | Intended Use |
|---|---|---|---|
| **Indian** | | | |
| ME 125 | 125 | 171 | mini |
| ME 100 | 100 | 162 | mini |
| ME 76 | 70 | 157 | mini |
| **Kawasaki** | | | |
| Z-1 900 | 900 | 505 | road |
| H-2 750 | 750 | 421 | road |
| S-2 350 | 350 | 336 | road |
| F-9 350 | 350 | 279 | dual |
| S-1 250 | 250 | 330 | road |
| F-11 250 | 250 | 262 | dual |
| F-7 175 | 175 | 232 | dual |
| F-6 125 | 125 | 230 | dual |
| G-5 100 | 100 | 196 | dual |
| MC-1 | 90 | 165 | mini |
| MT-1 | 75 | 120 | mini |
| **Maico** | | | |
| K501 | 501 | 238 | comp |
| K400 | 400 | 227 | comp |
| K250 | 250 | 220 | comp |
| K125/6 | 125 | 179 | comp |
| **Montesa** | | | |
| Cota 250 | 250 | 192 | comp |
| Cappra 250 VR | 250 | 211 | dual |
| King Scorpian | 250 | 238 | dual |
| Cappra 125 MX | 125 | 197 | comp |
| Cota 123 | 123 | 157 | comp |
| Cota 25 | 50 | 77 | mini |
| **Norton** | | | |
| Commando Roadster | 750 | 395 | road |
| Commando Interstate | 750 | 395 | road |
| Commando Racer | 750 | 385 | comp |
| **Ossa** | | | |
| Pioneer 250 | 250 | 235 | dual |
| Stiletto 250 | 250 | 233 | comp |
| Pioneer 175 | 175 | 235 | dual |
| **Penton** | | | |
| 175 Jack Piner | 175 | 246 | comp |
| 125 Six Day | 125 | 205 | comp |
| 100 Berkshire | 100 | 205 | comp |
| **Rickman** | | | |
| 250 Moto Cross | 250 | 203 | comp |
| 125 Enduro | 125 | 188 | dual |
| 125 Moto Cross | 125 | 180 | comp |
| **Rupp** | | | |
| RMT 80 | 80 | 135 | mini |
| **Suzuki** | | | |
| GT 750 LeMans | 750 | 508 | road |
| GT 550 Indy | 550 | 442 | road |
| T 500 Titan | 500 | 413 | road |

| Manufacturer Model | Engine Size c.c.'s | Weight lbs. | Intended Use |
|---|---|---|---|
| **Suzuki** | | | |
| TM 400 Cyclone | 400 | 236 | comp |
| TS 400 Apache | 400 | 278 | dual |
| GT 380 Sebring | 380 | 378 | road |
| GT 250 Hustler | 250 | 323 | road |
| TS 250 Savage | 250 | 246 | dual |
| TM 250 Champion | 250 | 221 | comp |
| TS 185 Sierra | 185 | 219 | dual |
| TC 125 Prospector | 125 | 210 | dual |
| TS 125 Duster | 125 | 199 | dual |
| TM 125 Challenger | 125 | 190 | comp |
| TC 100 Blazer | 100 | 206 | dual |
| TS 100 Honcho | 100 | 203 | dual |
| RV 90 Rover | 90 | 186 | mini |
| TS 50 Gaucho | 50 | 157 | mini |
| MT 50 Trailhopper | 50 | 133 | mini |
| **Triumph** | | | |
| Tiger TR7RV | 750 | 389 | road |
| Bonneville T140RV | 750 | 390 | road |
| Hurricane TRX75 | 740 | 458 | road |
| Trident T150V | 740 | 460 | road |
| Trophy Trail TR5T | 490 | 330 | dual |
| Daytona T100R | 490 | 356 | road |
| **Yamaha** | | | |
| TX 750 | 750 | 486 | road |
| TX 650 | 650 | 428 | road |
| SC 500 | 500 | 237 | comp |
| MX 360 | 350 | 235 | comp |
| RD 350 | 350 | 312 | road |
| RT3 | 350 | 263 | dual |
| RD 250 | 250 | 305 | road |
| DT3 | 250 | 259 | dual |
| MX 250 | 250 | 228 | comp |
| CT3 | 175 | 222 | dual |
| AT3 | 125 | 215 | dual |
| LT3 | 100 | 186 | dual |
| LT3MX | 100 | 186 | comp |
| GT-1 | 75 | 142 | mini |
| GT-1MX | 75 | 129 | mini |

This listing is intended to provide only a general picture of the different bikes that are available. Model designations change frequently—new models come along on a regular basis.

The only column that requires explanation is "Intended Use". ROAD means road **only**. DUAL covers bikes that can be ridden both on and off the road, though some may be much more at home in one or the other situation. COMP stands for competition and means that the bike is not street legal. Of the MINI bikes listed, some are equipped with lights, full fenders, a horn and other registration requirements. However, the wisdom of registering and riding them on the road is questionable. Others in the MINI group are for trail and field use, or competition.

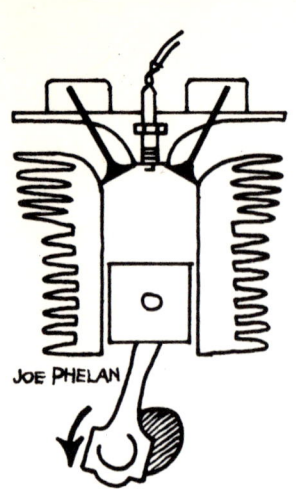

JOE PHELAN

# WHY IT WORKS

There is a section in this book about repairing motorcycles. It will help you perform some of the ordinary maintenance related to riding, and keeping your bike in good condition. It will also give you a fairly good idea of the tools you'll need and the most effective ways to use them. What the section on repair won't give you is a detailed step-by-step procedure for specific major repairs. Here's why.

Though there isn't anything very mysterious about an engine overhaul or rebuilding a transmission, they are complicated jobs. Before attempting a job like that, you need a thorough understanding of what you're doing. And before you can know how something works, or how to fix it, you should know why it should work in the first place. If you start with the basic understanding of why a particular part of an engine is there, and what it does in relation to the rest of the engine, you'll soon be able to see why the engine runs.

All mechanical things are the same in one respect. No matter how complex or complicated they become in their finished appearance, they all started with basic principles that never vary. There are some fundamental reasons why they work. Let's apply that thinking to an engine and see what happens.

Combustion, or the burning of fuel, is the basis for power in any engine. Burning occurs when three things are present: something to burn (fuel), something to support the burning (oxygen), and something to start the burning (ignition). In a gasoline engine the fuel will be gasoline (natch!). The best source of oxygen is the atmosphere around us, so air is used. The mixture of fuel and air will be ignited by an electrical spark, provided by an electrical system, which all engines have to one degree or another. If one of these elements (fuel, air, ignition) is missing, there can be no burning. You can prove this by putting a candle in a jar, lighting it, and closing the jar. When the oxygen is used by the burning, the candle goes out. When a mixture of gasoline and air is ignited, it begins to expand. If the burning, and resulting expansion, is contained, pressure is built up inside the container, and that pressure can be used to do the work.

The container that we'll use is a cylinder with one end closed. Inside the cylinder is a piston that is free to slide back and forth. The piston fits the cylinder very closely to keep the pressure from escaping. Now if combustion takes place inside the cylinder, the pressure (expansion) will try to force the piston out, and it is at this point that a very important thing is happening. Chemical energy, the burning of the air/fuel vapors, is being changed to mechanical energy, the force exerted by the piston, on whatever we connect it to. A rod called (of all things) a connecting rod gets attached to the outside end of the piston, and to a crankshaft. Through this arrangement the sliding piston can be made to do some useful work. The crankshaft is the device that is used to receive and deliver the power and to get the piston back up inside the cyclinder.

A second important change is taking place at this point, The back-and-forth (reciprocating) motion of the piston is being changed to a circular or rotary motion. (Note: This shouldn't be confused with rotary engines, as they operate on a principle which eliminates the sliding piston altogether.) The circular motion of the crankshaft will eventually wind up on the road, put there by the wheel that drives the vehicle.

A simple way to illustrate this change from reciprocating to rotary motion is to compare it to a pedal bike. The knee of the rider is our piston, his leg is the connecting rod, and the pedal/sprocket of the bicycle represents the crankshaft. The knee goes up and down, the sprocket goes around, and through the use of a chain the back wheel transfers the motion to the road.

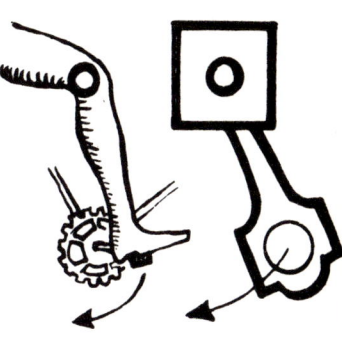

To keep the engine running, there must be more than just one movement of the piston. This is solved by exhausting burned gases and supplying a fresh mixture to be ignited. It is here that motorcycle engines vary in design. Let's say that each time there is burning in the cylinder a power cycle has been completed. That cycle will have included getting the fuel/air mixture into the cylinder, igniting it, using the outward motion of the piston to do work, and emptying the cylinder. Each time the piston moves in either direction it is called a stroke.

In one type of motorcycle engine, the power cycle is completed in two piston strokes, while in the other type four piston strokes are needed to complete the power cycle. From this we get the terms two-stroke and four-stroke engines. Engines can also be referred to as two-cycle or four-cycle. Those terms are really abbreviations of two or four "stroke power cycle." The four-stroke engine is the easier of the two to learn on, because only one thing happens on each stroke.

Initially, the gas/air mix must get into the cylinder. This is accomplished through the use of a valve in the top of the cylinder. When the piston is at the top of its travel, the intake valve opens, and the piston begins to move down. As it does, the mixture of gasoline and air is drawn in after it. As the piston reaches the bottom of its travel, the intake valve closes, and the intake stroke (the first stroke of the four) is completed. The piston begins to rise again, and the mixture of gas and air is compressed. This is actually the basic reason that the engine runs. If the mixture were not compressed, the burning would not be intense, and the piston would not be in a position to use the power developed by the burning.

When the piston reaches the top of its travel, the compression stroke (the second of the four) is completed. Now ignition begins. An electrical spark is made to jump across a gap between two metal rods called electrodes. The electrodes are simply the business ends of the spark

## 4 CYCLE ENGINE OPERATION

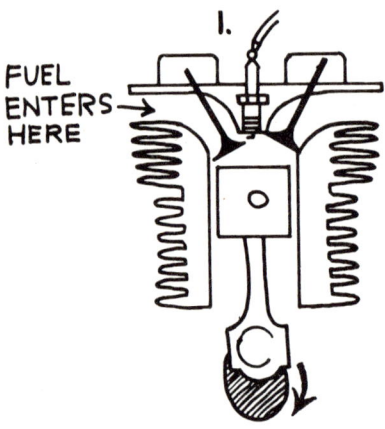

INTAKE STROKE- INTAKE VALVE OPENS- PISTON MOVES DOWN- DRAWS IN MIXTURE

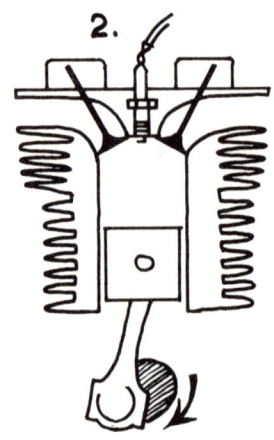

COMPRESSION STROKE- INTAKE VALVE CLOSES- PISTON MOVES UP- COMPRESSES MIXTURE

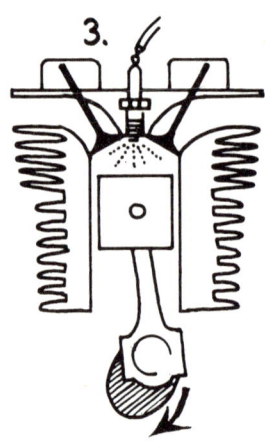

POWER STROKE- SPARK PLUG IGNITES MIXTURE- PUSHES PISTON DOWN

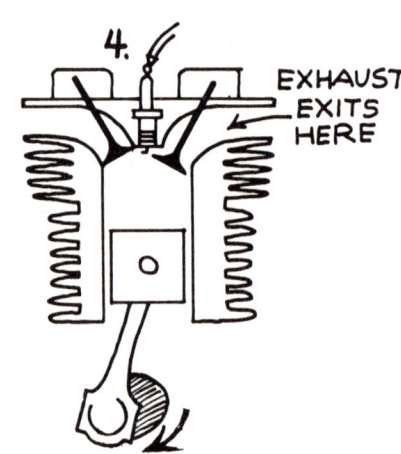

EXHAUST STROKE- EXHAUST VALVE OPENS- PISTON MOVES UP- FORCES BURNED MIXTURE OUT

plug, which is the last stage of the electrical system. The spark starts the mixture burning and expanding, which forces the piston down again on the power stroke. When the piston reaches bottom, the power stroke (the third of four) is complete and the exhaust stroke (the fourth and final) begins.

Back up at the top of the cylinder, another valve, the exhaust valve, is opening. As the piston rises, the burned mixture is forced out of the cylinder until, at the top of the exhaust stroke, the exhaust valve closes, which completes the power cycle. Before the piston moves down again, the intake valve opens, and another power cycle begins.

Before we go too much further, let's put together a simple engine.

# 2 CYCLE ENGINE OPERATION

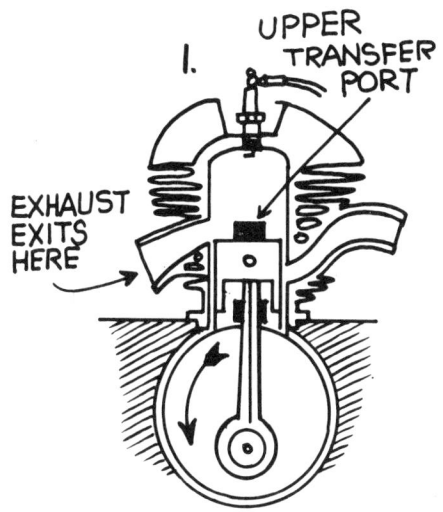

PISTON FALLS - FRESH FUEL ENTERS FROM UPPER TRANSFER PORT AND FORCES OLD MIXTURE OUT OF EXHAUST PORT

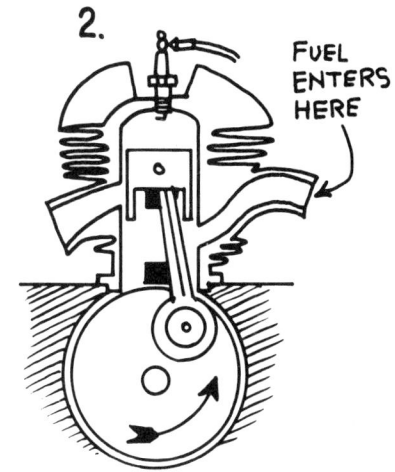

PISTON RISES - FRESH FUEL IS COMPRESSED - EXHAUST PORT IS SEALED - NEW FUEL ENTERS CRANKCASE AREA

MIXTURE IGNITES - PRODUCES POWER - PISTON IS FORCED DOWN AND SEALS UPPER TRANFER PORT

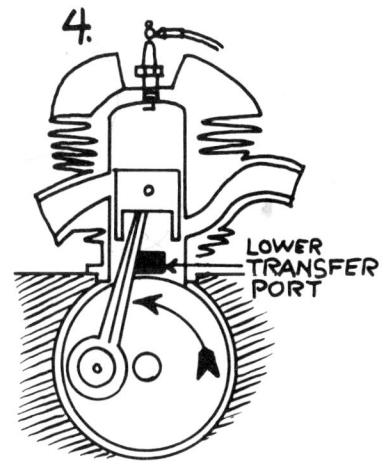

FALLING PISTON CLOSES INTAKE PORT AND COMPRESSES MIXTURE IN CRANKCASE - MIXTURE ENTERS LOWER TRANSFER PORT

The crankshaft is mounted in a crankcase. The crankshaft turns in bearings that are lubricated by oil, which is either stored in the crankcase or in a tank located elsewhere.

One end of the crankshaft will be used to transmit the power that the engine develops to the driving wheel, and the other end will drive the cams. The cams, you say, who are the cams? Well, they're the guys who tell the valves when to open and close. That's necessary because the valves have to move when the piston needs them to. So, because the piston is connected to the crankshaft, it makes sense that the valves should be, too. This is accomplished through a set of gears, and though the arrangement varies from engine to engine, the principle is universal

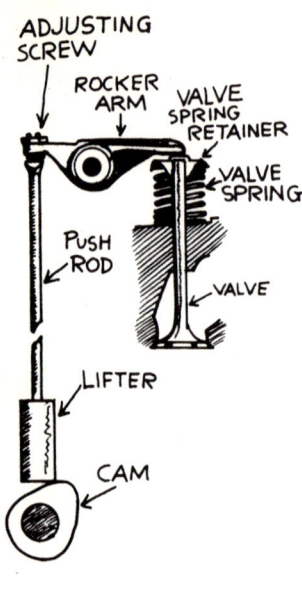

to all four strokes. The cams are part of a shaft which is also mounted in bearings. The shaft is called a camshaft. Each cam is egg-shaped, so that, as it turns, it will lift whatever is put on top of it.

What's on top is a little barrel called a valve lifter. On top of the lifter sits a push rod, which operates a lever called a rocker arm. The other end of the rocker arm pushes down on the top of the valve. The bottom end of the valve ends up in the cylinder. A spring around the upper portion of the valve stem closes the valve and keeps the push rod and the lifter riding firmly on the cam. The different parts that operate the valves can be singularly referred to as the valve train.

The difference between four-stroke and two-stroke engines is found in the number of piston strokes per power cycle. In a four-stroke engine, the piston must move three separate times for each power stroke it delivers: intake, compression, power, exhaust. Two-stroke engines deliver a power stroke each time the piston travels down, and they do this by combining the separate things that happen in a four-stroke. Reciprocating (back-and-forth) valve trains are absent in two-strokes, the intake and exhaust processes being handled by the piston which moves past ports in the sides of the cylinder. Further, the crankcase area plays an important part in the two-stroke power cycle.

The intake port, through which the fuel/air mixture enters, is located low in the cylinder, and is covered when the piston is at the bottom of its travel. As the piston rises, the intake port is uncovered and, because the crankcase area is sealed, a vacuum is created by the rising piston. The vacuum draws in the mixture. The piston continues to rise, and as it does, it seals the upper outlet of the transfer port, which is a passageway outside the cylinder through which the fresh gas/air mixture from the last cycle has been passing into the compression area above the piston. That fresh mixture, by the way, was also clearing the spent gases from the cylinder, by forcing them through an exhaust port, which was uncovered when the piston was at the bottom of its travel. As the piston reaches the top of its travel, a spark occurs at the spark plug and a power stroke begins.

As the piston travels downward, it seals the intake port. Its downward motion also begins to force the fresh fuel/air mixture, which has just entered the crankcase, into the lower opening of the transfer port. The piston continues downward and uncovers the upper transfer port. Mixture enters and exhausts the gases that have just been burned.

The thing that can make a two-stroke hard to understand is its simplicity, but if you read back over the text and study the drawings, the system should become clear.

Because the crackcase area is used as an integral part of the power cycle, it cannot be used to hold lubricating oil. For this reason, and because the rotating parts must be lubricated, oil is mixed with the gasoline. The oil travels with the gasoline/air mix through the crankcase, lubricating as it goes, and is burned with the mixture.

There are variations on the ways the gas/air/oil mixture enters the cylinder, but the principle of two-stroke operation remains the same.

We've been talking all along about mixing gas and air without really knowing how we're doing it. A thing called a carburetor handles that chore, and is also responsible for determining the speed at which the engine runs. Engine speed, as long as I brought it up, is measured in revolutions of the crankshaft over a period of a minute. An engine speed of 1,000 rpm's (revolutions per minute) means that the crankshaft revolves a thousand times in one minute.

It is interesting to note that if we apply this to a two-stroke engine, it means that there will be 500 power strokes in the minute, while a four-stroke engine will produce only 250 power strokes in the same period of time. This does not, however, have as much to do with the amount of power either engine produces as it does with the way the power is delivered to the wheel.

Back to carburetors. Air has weight. You don't think of it that way because you can't see it, or feel it, but it has weight, nonetheless. Because it has weight, air exerts pressure on everything it touches, you and me included.

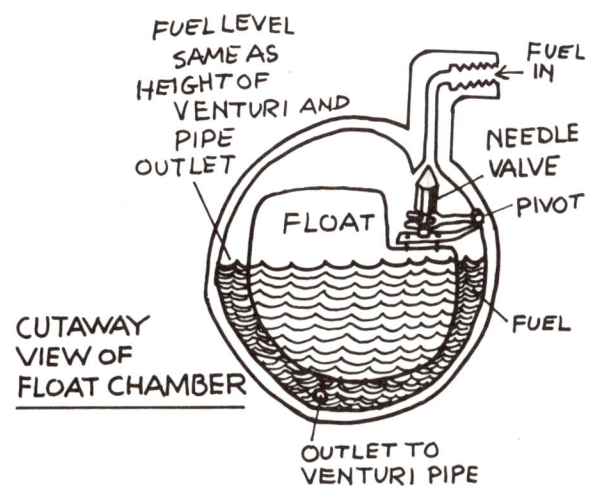

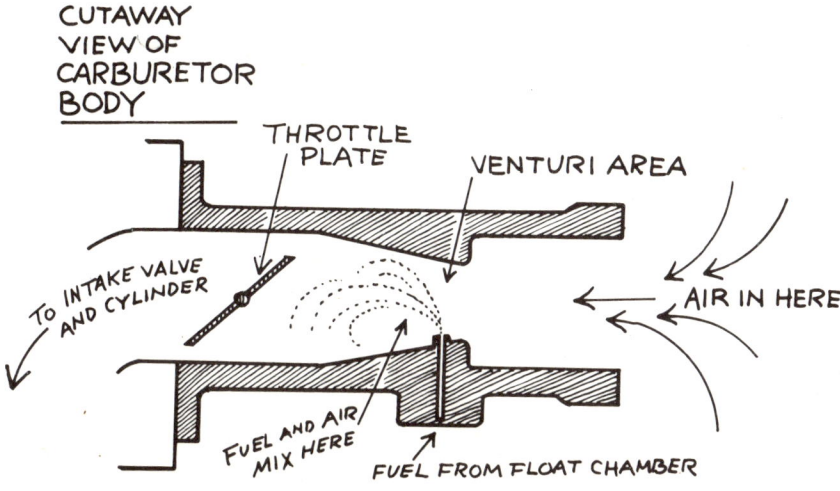

Maybe this will be clearer if you think about what happens when you put your arm out the window of a moving car. You feel resistance, right? That's because your arm is displacing the air that occupied the space your arm is in now, before you got there. The air is exerting pressure on your arm.

Air pressure is measured at sea level and expressed in pounds per square inch. Normal air pressure at sea level is 14.7 pounds per square inch. Unless something happens to lower the pressure of air, there is no movement of air, but because there are constant changes in air pressure all over the world, there is always a flow of air going on. Result, wind.

Whether you know it or not, when you drink through a straw, you are using air pressure. Without thinking about it, you enlarge the capacity of your lungs, which creates a vacuum. Since now there is more room in your lungs, and the same amount of air, the air pressure in your lungs is lower than the pressure of the air outside your body, which is pushing down on the liquid in the glass. Because this is so, normal outside air pressure forces the liquid up the straw and into your mouth. (Your body automatically keeps the liquid from going into your lungs.)

Carburetors are a bit like straws in that they rely on unequal air pressure to do their job. When a piston moves down in a cylinder, it creates a vacuum.

The carburetor is connected between the cylinder and the outside air, so air rushing into the cylinder to fill the vacuum passes through the carburetor. That accounts for how the air gets there. In the case of a motorcycle, gasoline relies on gravity.

The gas tank is higher than the carburetor, so the gas flows out and down. A flexible hose (rubber or plastic) runs from the tank to the carburetor, more specifically, to the float chamber of the carburetor. Take the top cover off a toilet tank, flush it, and you'll see how a float chamber works. It's basically a storage tank with a valve that meters quantities of liquid. When the liquid falls below a predetermined level, the valve opens and allows more liquid to enter the chamber. The flow of liquid is checked by a needle and seat arrangement, and the amount of liquid going in is determined by the amount of liquid going out. And in the case of the carburetor, the amount of liquid going out is determined by air pressure. Here's how it happens.

Air, passing through the carburetor, changes speed at a point called the venturi. Think of the carburetor as a pipe, and the venturi as a point inside the pipe where the opening rapidly grows smaller, as though it had been pinched. After that point, it gradually grows larger until it reaches its original size. That change of shape causes an increase in the velocity of the air passing through the opening, which results in a lessening in air pressure just after the point where the carburetor got smaller. It is at this point of pressure change that a tube from the float bowl lets gasoline enter the airstream.

The faster the air passes through the venturi, the lower the air pressure after the venturi will be. The greater the pressure difference between the venturi area and normal air pressure, or the pressure in the float chamber, the faster the gasoline in the tube will be drawn into the airstream.

The speed of the mixture's passage through the carburetor and the resulting amount of gas/air mix delivered to the cylinder is governed by the throttle, which is a plate that closes across the carburetor opening, past the point where the fuel and air mix. Closing or opening the throttle regulates the amount of vacuum applied to the outside air. The vacuum, of course, is constant, since it is caused by the descending piston. But its effect on the atmosphere can be, and is, changed by the throttle.

The throttle is connected, in the case of a motorcycle, to the right handlebar grip. In a car, the other end of the throttle is the gas pedal.

Some carburetors have in place of the plate/venturi arrangement, a slide that moves back and forth across the path of the air. This regulates the speed of the air over the fuel inlet opening and, consequently, the amount of fuel that is drawn into the airstream. The principle here is much like a perfume bottle with a rubber bulb. When the bulb is squeezed, air is rapidly forced to pass over a tube that leads to the perfume, causing a low-pressure condition in the tube, and drawing the liquid out.

We have the piston in the right place, and we have the air/fuel mix in the cylinder where it belongs. All we need is a spark, and the engine will run. Electrical systems are, of course, used for other things than running the engine, but for now we'll only concern ourselves with getting a spark to the spark plug.

The source of electricity can vary. Sometimes a magneto or an alternator acts as the source. The traditional power supply, however, has been the wet-cell storage battery. A chemical reaction between two

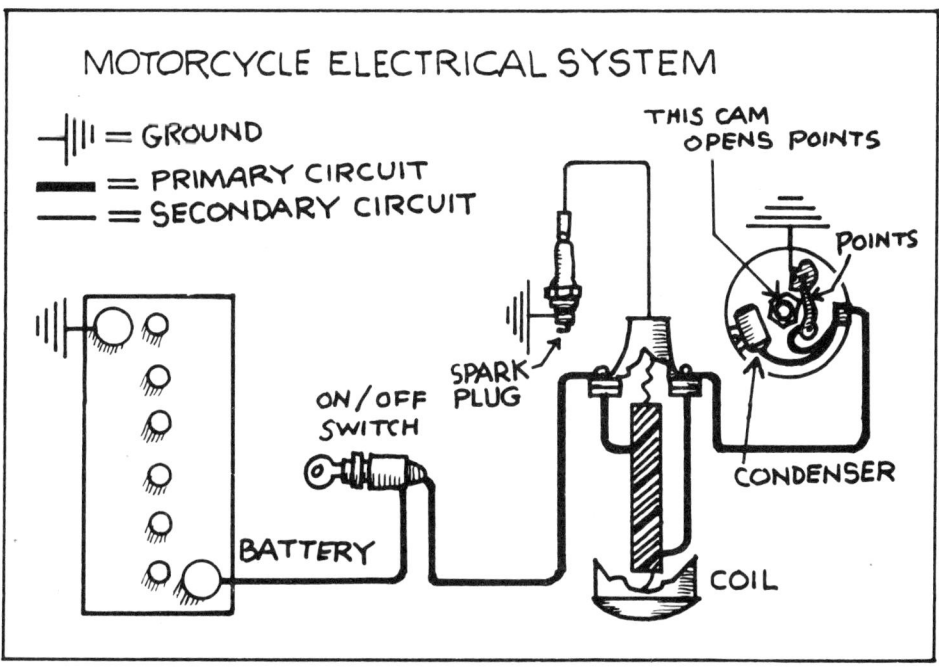

35

different types of metal plates and acid produces electricity in the battery. Half of the plates are positively charged and half are negatively charged. The terminals outside the battery are the end connections of the different sets of plates. One terminal is positive, one negative. If we connect something between the terminals, electricity will flow through whatever we have used as a connector—provided, that is, that the connector will conduct electricity in the first place. Wire and metal conduct electricity. Rubber and wood do not. The thing that is important to remember is that unless there is some way for electricity to get back to the battery, it will not leave.

Unless there is a complete circuit between the positive and negative terminals, nothing happens. One way to insure that something will happen is to use the chassis of the vehicle as a conductor. One terminal of the battery, usually the negative one, is connected to the chassis with a cable. It thus establishes a ground, or a place for electricity to go after it has done work. The other terminal, with cables and wires, is connected to all the things that need to get electrical power. Those things are, in turn, connected to the chassis, and so to ground. This is usually accomplished by bolting the particular part to the chassis or to something that is bolted to the chassis. Additionally, there can be grounding straps connecting parts to the chassis.

There are different ways to rate the power of electricity. In the ignition system, we are concerned with voltage. If you think of electricity flowing through a circuit as water flowing through a pipe, voltage is the pressure pushing it through. Automotive and motorcycle batteries are either six- or twelve-volt batteries, ample for lighting the lights and blowing the horn, but not for firing the spark plug. It takes from 20,000 to 25,000 volts to make a spark jump between the electrodes, so a method of increasing the voltage must be used. This is done by something called a coil, and in motorcycle ignition systems there is one coil for each spark plug.

There are two separate circuits in the ignition system. One is called the primary circuit. The primary circuit is directly connected to the battery and carries the low voltage (6 or 12 volts) from the battery to the coil, generally through a switch which is used to turn the system on and off. The secondary circuit begins in the coil, and is the high-voltage circuit which supplies the 20,000 to 25,000 volts to the spark plug.

The coil itself is really two coils of wire. The primary circuit enters the coil and winds around an iron center post several hundred times. It then leaves the coil and goes somewhere else. The secondary circuit begins in the coil with windings that number in the several thousands. These secondary windings are wound over the primary windings, but are insulated from the primary so that there is no physical connection between the primary and secondary circuits.

The secondary circuit continues from the coil to the top of the spark plug and down through the center of the plug to the center electrode. At this point there is a gap across which the electricity will jump. There is another electrode there which is connected to the thread portion of the spark plug, and so to ground. That completes the secondary circuit.

Now, that wire that left the primary windings of the coil has to go somewhere. Eventually, it works its way back to ground, but not before passing through a switch which has one stationary contact that is grounded by the bolts that hold it in place, and another contact that is insulated from the first one, and is movable. When the switch is closed, the primary circuit is complete and current flows to ground. When the switch is open, no current will flow. The switch is operated by a revolving cam which, through a series of gears, is connected to the camshaft, which you remember is connected to the crankshaft. As the crankshaft turns, the switch opens and closes. The opening of the switch is timed to occur as the piston is getting ready for a power stroke.

With the switch closed, electricity is flowing in the primary circuit, and those primary windings in the coil are creating a magnetic field around the iron post. When the switch opens, the primary circuit is broken, and the magnetic field collapses. When this happens, a high voltage is created in the secondary portion of the coil, because of the great difference between the number of primary and secondary windings. The high voltage travels to the spark plug and ignites the mixture. The power stroke begins.

This actually happens just slightly before the piston reaches the top of its travel, to make sure that the mixture will have enough time to burn thoroughly and exert maximum pressure on the piston.

The switch, with its contact points, is referred to as the points. It must be adjusted to open to a specific distance and at a specific time.

One of the properties of electricity is its tendency to keep flowing. When a circuit is broken, there is a tiny fraction of a second when current tries to jump across the break, and an arc of electricity can occur. In an ignition system, the points are opening and closing all the time—breaking the flow of electricity, and creating a potential for arcing between the contacts of the points. Because it is important for the primary field to collapse at a precise time, the points must open with a minimum of arcing. In other words, the current must be shut off as abruptly as possible. A device called a condenser is used to aid in this process. The condenser catches the electricity that is trying to jump across the points, and stores it until the points have opened far enough to prevent arcing on their own. The condenser then releases the stored electricity to ground.

A motorcycle that has more than one cylinder can either have a set of points for each cylinder, or multiple lobes on the cam that operate one set and points. In any case, there will be one coil per cylinder. In a car, a spark gets handed out by a rotor which receives the current from one coil, spins around, and distributes it to as many spark-plug wires as need it.

That's all there is. That's all it takes to make an engine run. Naturally, all these things have to happen at the right time, and all the parts must be adjusted properly, but knowing why something works gets you more than halfway toward keeping it working properly.

# NUTS, BOLTS, SCREWS, HAMMERS, PLIERS, AND FIXES

No matter how well a mechanical thing is designed or how well it is manufactured, it is only a mechanical thing and will eventually need to be repaired. Motorcycles are mechanical things. Very personal, very private, but very mechanical things. They break, and there are two people who can fix them—you and somebody else. This chapter is here because not every repair, or adjustment, has to be done by somebody else. Much can be done by the rider, and he doesn't have to be a wizard with a wrench, or have a total understanding of mechanics.

Before you begin an adjustment or repair, you should have (1) the necessary tools to do the work, (2) an understanding of the work that you're going to do, and (3) the correct parts (in the case of repair) to complete the work.

Let's start small and at the beginning. Because every mechanical thing you'll come across, as long as you do any type of maintenance or repair, will be held together with nuts or bolts or screws, understanding them is helpful.

Most of the nuts you'll encounter will have six flats, as will the heads of most bolts. Screws can be either of two types, common or Phillips. Common screws have a slot across the head while Phillips screws have an "x" pattern there.

There is a third fastener which might be considered either a screw or a bolt. It's called an allen screw, and the tool used to install or remove it is an allen wrench. Allen screws have six-sided holes in their heads. Not surprisingly, allen wrenches are six-sided rods which are bent to form an "L." This kind of screw (bolt) can be drawn more tightly than other kinds of screws.

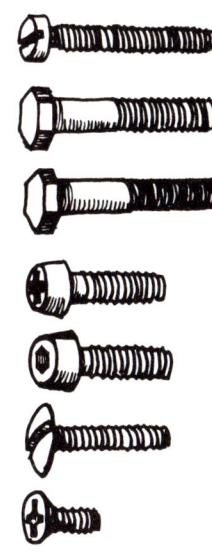

A couple of general rules: If a nut or bolt is dirty, clean it before you use it. If the threads are damaged, or the flats are rounded off, don't use it. In fact, throw it away. Bad threads can only lead to more bad threads, and rounded corners will make it difficult (if not impossible) to remove the next time.

O.K., how tight is tight? Well, that's not too easy to explain, but realize this. It is possible to strip the threads out of nuts and off bolts by overtightening. One way to avoid this is to use a logical tool. Don't put a twelve-inch adjustable wrench on a 1/4" nut and turn as hard as you can. Something will break, and it won't be the wrench. Also, look out for different metals. Metals like aluminum (lots of it is used on bikes) and brass (used mostly in gas- or oil-line fittings) are much softer than steel, and therefore much more likely to be damaged by heavy-handed wrenching. Is that all there is to know about nuts and bolts? Not really, but it should be enough to get you started, and keep you out of trouble for a while.

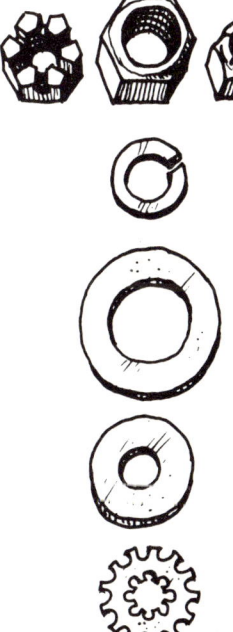

Now, about tools and which ones you're going to need. Start by looking at whatever came with the bike. There will probably be a screwdriver of some sort, probably two, but don't plan on being able to use them in any but the simplest of places. There will be a plug wrench. It will most likely be tube-like with a bar that fits through two holes in one end. Unless it looks like it's going to break the first time you use it, hang on to it. This kind of plug tool is perfectly adequate for most bikes, and it doesn't take up that much space. It's a good tool to keep with the bike. You'll see why the first time you have to change a plug on the road, and you don't have a wrench. Incidentally, the only thing worse than not having the wrench is having the wrench and not having a plug. So wrap some cloth around the top portion of a fresh plug that you have wisely already gapped, and put it inside the wrench. The cloth keeps the plug from banging around inside the wrench, which could crack the porcelain and make the plug worthless. Of course, you can sometimes clean fouled plugs on the road, but it means carrying the things to do it with. In any case, if you want to try to use a plug again, it's a lot easier to do your cleaning at home.

Other things that might be in the tool kit when you get the bike are: thickness gauges, tire irons, a wrench to adjust rear spring/shock absorber units, and other wrenches. These will be (hopefully) the things needed to handle most roadside repairs. Rarely, however, is the tool kit that comes with most bikes complete enough to tackle the jobs that the rider is capable of handling himself. If he wants to do his own work, he buys some tools.

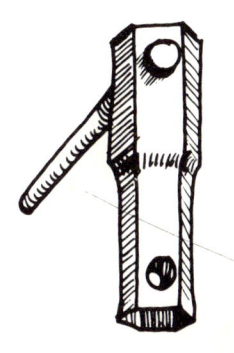

What you buy, as I said, depends largely on how much of your own work you want to do, and it will take a little time to determine that. When you do buy a tool, buy one that will last awhile. It makes more sense to spend $5.00 once, on a high-quality version of something, than to spend $2.00 three or four times replacing a tool that keeps wearing out or breaking. This does not mean that you have to buy "top-of-the-line" tools, but rather that if you buy at bargain prices, you are probably going to get unhappy fast.

Don't worry about not having a selection. There are several manufacturers of acceptable-quality, reasonably priced hand tools. Ask your bike dealer what auto supply stores carry tools, or check the Yellow Pages. For that matter, any mechanic will be able to tell you where to buy tools.

When you do buy, ask if there is a guarantee. Sometimes there is. Of course, it won't cover misuse, and good tools don't break that often, but it's good to know about.

Tools can be purchased two ways, individually, and in sets (example: all the wrenches from 5 to 15 mm's). Usually, the price per tool is about the same, but here, too, there can be exceptions. You'll have to look around if you have a tight budget. There are advantages either way. When you buy on a one-at-a-time basis, you probably never own a tool that you don't use. When you buy in sets, you rarely get stuck not having a tool when you need it. It's up to you. One approach to the problem is to take a good, long look at your bike. Spend an afternoon measuring nuts and bolts. The object is to find out which sizes are the most common. Buy your tools accordingly. See how many of the screws are Phillips. How many are common? What size screwdrivers are you going to need?

Now, what are you going to buy? Screwdrivers. They're measured in blade length, and come in three types: Phillips, common (which we know about), and cabinet. Common and cabinet screwdrivers are practically the same, with the exception that the blade of a cabinet screwdriver doesn't widen. It's the same width from tip to the handle, while a common screwdriver widens just after the tip. Cabinet screwdrivers can be useful in situations where you're working with screws that countersink into castings. It's important to use the proper-size screwdriver, and that's determined by the head of the screw. When using common or cabinet screwdrivers, the tip of the blade should be as close to the width of the screw as possible. In the case of Phillips screws, try to match the drive point closely to the screw. Apply pressure evenly and in line with the screw. You can be tempted to use a screwdriver for other things. This temptation will result in a bent or broken tool, skinned knuckles, or a damaged part. The right tool for the job is the right tool.

Pliers, another tool that's usually asked to do more than it's supposed to. They're for holding, generally, and they make lousy wrenches and worse hammers. You can use them for tightening. Go right ahead, but

finish with a wrench. There are several kinds of plier(s). Standard pliers will comfortably handle nuts or bolts up to about 1-1/4". Sizes larger than that force the handles too far apart for your hand to grasp properly. Variable-jar pliers, sometimes called waterpump pliers, can be adjusted to handle sizes up to around 3", and some are bigger. I can't think of any motorcycle application for anything that size, except perhaps axle nuts or bearing race nuts, and those had better be worked on with wrenches.

As soon as I said I couldn't think of things, I started to do just that, but in each case, a wrench was the better tool by far. Needlenose pliers are pretty well described by their name. Their long, tapering jaws hold small nuts in hard-to-reach places. They're like heavy-duty tweezers and are also handy for working with wire. Side cutting pliers aren't really pliers. They're scissors for wire, but they work like pliers.

Vice Grips. They're as close to a wrench as a pair of pliers can come. They are adjustable through their range of opening and they lock onto whatever they're holding. They aren't foolproof. They can slip. To work effectively, vice grips need a good, clean bite, and they must be set properly, but don't be afraid to use them. They are the ultimate pliers since pliers are for holding. Try hard not to use pliers on things that you don't want scratched. Pliers' jaws can really make a mess out of a chrome exhaust pipe.

Wrenches come in as many different sizes and shapes as you'd want, yet there are only two basic patterns. The jaws of an open-end wrench form a "U." The distance inside the jaws is what determines the size of the wrench, and that's based upon the size of the bolt or nut the wrench is supposed to be for. Not confusing, is it? Box wrenches are really more like circles, since the jaw surrounds the bolt or nut. The inside of the box (circle) is machined to the size of the bolt or nut and has six flats. Here's a twist (no pun). Some box wrenches have no flats. They have dents which fit over the points of the bolt or nut. Described as twelve-point wrenches, they're sometimes more convenient in close quarters because they're able to grab the bolt or nut in more places. By the way, box wrenches with six flats are also called six-point wrenches.

On to combination wrenches. Box on one end, open-end on the other. They're offset for knuckle room. Both the box and the open-end are the same size. Double-box wrenches are offset, too, but have different size boxes. Double open-end wrenches are also two different sizes.

As far as wrenching rules go, just remember that the only wrench to use is one that's the same size as the bolt you are working on. Obviously, you won't be able to use one that's too small, but it is possible to use one that's just a little too big. When the wrench slips (which it will), rounded points and battered fingers result. Don't hammer on wrenches. Don't put extensions on them. The length of a given wrench is generally adequate to insure plenty of leverage without help. Try to do final tightening with a six-point wrench. You'll have more control, less chance of slippage, and a better feel of how tight

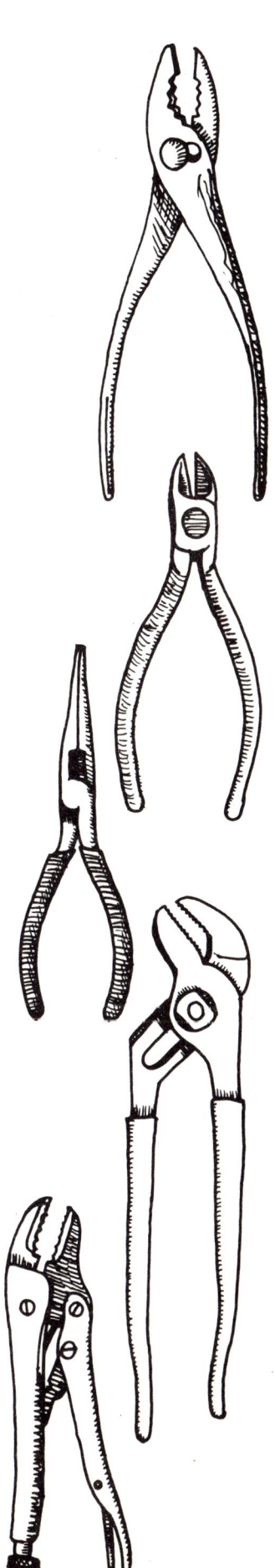

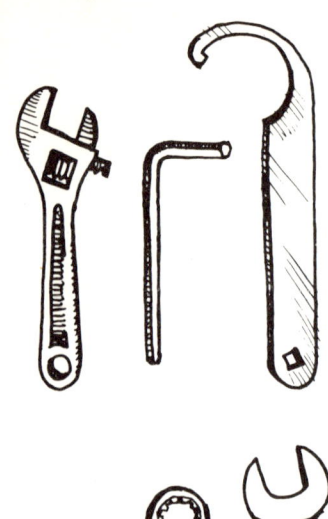

you're tightening. A beginning wrench set might include double-box and open-end wrenches from 1/4" to 7/8", or in mm's, from about 5 to 24.

Another valuable item is an adjustable wrench. It falls into the open-end category, but one jaw moves, and you can set any size or fraction thereof that you want. Although they're bulkier than open-end, they can be useful for blind work. Again, try to do final tightening with a box wrench.

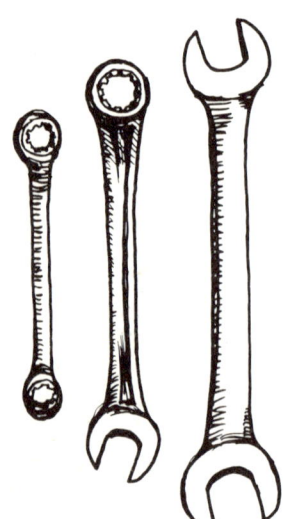

Sockets are really timesavers. They fit a reversible ratchet handle, and are like a box wrench in pattern. They also come in six- or twelve-point design. They are identified by the size nut or bolt they fit and by the size of the handle's drive bit. The drive sizes you'll run into are 1/4", 3/8", and 1/2". A 3/8" set drive will cope with just about everything but the smallest or largest nuts and bolts, and is probably the best bet for a beginner. The sockets available range from 3/8" (you can probably find a 1/4" socket for a 3/8" drive if you need it) to 7/8" Also, if you think you need to, you might be able to find larger ones or get an adapter to use 1/2" drive sockets. Sockets are also available in metric sizes and fit standard handles. You can get all sorts of accessories. Screwdriver bits, allen bits and universal joints which, when used with an extension, allow you to work at an angle. Deep-set sockets let you run a nut down a long bolt, and there are special spark-plug sockets, with rubber grabbers inside, which hold the plug. Here, a note of caution. Always start a spark plug by hand and make sure that the threads are properly aligned before you begin to tighten it with a wrench. This is especially true when the cylinder head is made of aluminum. Like one on a motorcycle? You bet!

You can get a screwdriver handle that will fit your sockets. If you have to start a bolt or nut in a place where your fingers won't go, put a little putty (or something similar) right into the socket and press the nut or bolt in to the top of the putty. Then use the handle driver to aim the nut or bolt where you want it. By the way, this trick also works with screws.

Hammers? A plastic or rubber one, and a ball-peen type, should be about it. In mechanics, hammers are for tapping. If you have to hit harder, something is wrong somewhere else. Ball peen hammers have the traditional hammerhead on one side and a ball (surprise!) on the other. The ball can be used to make gaskets. If you place gasket material on the part that needs the gasket, and tap gently, the material will tear around the edges of the part. If you do it with patience, using great care to hit just hard enough, but not too hard, you'll have a nice gasket. By the time you do it, however, very often you've wasted as much time as the whole job would have taken if you had used a ready-made gasket. Making gaskets is a tinkerer's delight. Don't try to make any but the simplest of gaskets; in fact, forget trying to make them at all. It's probably the wisest "forget" you'll ever do. Plastic or rubber hammers can be used effectively as a means of jarring loose balky parts, and chrome or polished metal won't be scratched. If it doesn't move after a couple of taps, before you hit it any harder, please make sure that all the bolts or nuts are accounted for. You'll be surprised at how often there's one just sitting there as tight as can be.

These tools just about complete a basic tool kit. But remember, you don't have to run down to buy all these things at once. Think about what work you want to do, and buy accordingly. There are some things that might come in handy that don't fall into the "must have" group. For instance, if for some reason, you have to put a new link in your bike's drive chain, you'll first have to get the bad link off. You could go through an elaborate procedure with a file and a lot of coaxing, or you could use a chain breaker. It's a little device made just for the job. Before you buy one, know what size chain you have. Your dealer should know. A pair of tire irons (you may already have them in the tool kit that came with the bike) is really the only way to go. Screwdrivers are out, because its too easy to pinch the tube, or tear up the bead of the tire. Thickness gauges. A blade type for points and valve adjustment, and a wire type for plugs. You can survive with just the blade, but if you want spot-on plug settings (and who doesn't?), the wire gauge is the one. This is especially true if you're regapping used plugs.

In the "nice-to-have" category is a putty knife. Use the kind with a blade about one inch wide. They are great for scraping old gaskets, but don't keep them too sharp, or you'll find yourself gouging away chunks of aluminum. Add tweezers, a magnet, a ruler, and a pencil or crayon, and you're all set.

Where do you keep all of this stuff? Good question. The logical answer, of course, is in a toolbox. But wait. There are more sizes, shapes, and prices of toolboxes than you'd imagine, and in terms of quality they range from absolutely unacceptable to "you'll-never-need-it-so-good." Wait awhile before you buy one. Ask questions, and pay attention to people when they say things like, "It was fine until it fell off the bench. Now it won't close right." Most of all, don't buy a box until your tool buying has leveled off. Even if you have to keep what tools you have in a cardboard box, you're better off doing that than buying two tool boxes, because the first one was too small. Remember, too, that neatness counts, and there's no point in jamming your tools into places that you have to unload each time you want the wrench that lives in the back.

There are really only two reasons to fix something. One is, something broke. Two is, if you don't fix it, it will break. The latter is preferable. What that means is, you're better off fixing something before it breaks than after it breaks, and that includes flat tires, fouled spark plugs, and broken drive chains. The list goes on. If you can get into the habit of checking things that could go wrong and making sure that they don't, you will never find yourself stranded. I suppose I should say, practically never. There's always the exception to the rule.

Let's assume, though, that the object is to prevent as much from

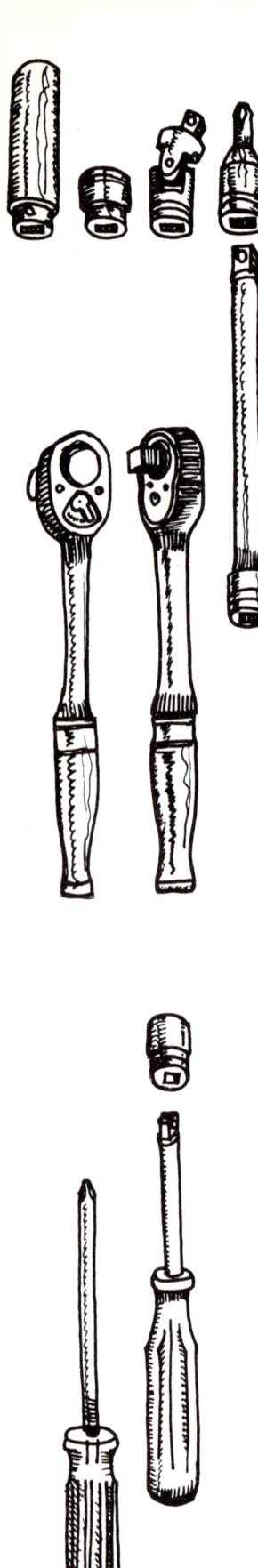

going wrong as is possible. The first thing to do is to get another tool. Sorry, but it's true. This tool—and, by the way, you may already have it—is absolutely invaluable. Every motorcycle ever made has some sort of owner's handbook. Don't make a move without it. If you don't have it, get it. It has information that you, as a maintainer of your own motorcycle, can't do without. Later on, you can pick up the factory manual, which covers every repair possible. For now, the owner's handbook should tell you what you need to know. Dealers carry or can get handbooks for you. Also, elsewhere in this book, there are addresses for manufacturers and distributors. Spend some time getting familiar with the owner's handbook. Besides information on the operation of your bike, it will contain the mechanical specifications and procedures you need for maintenance, and because it's written for the rider (whom the manufacturer assumes is not a mechanic), it is fairly easy to understand.

Whether you are changing a tire or adjusting valves, there is a right way to begin. Start by making sure that the part of the bike you're going to work on, the area you're going to work in, your tools, and your hands are clean. I don't necessarily mean sterile, but at least free from grease and dirt. Working this way not only makes the job more pleasant, but it keeps dirt from getting into places that it shouldn't. Of course, if you keep your bike and tools clean all the time, you're halfway there.

Work out a "game plan" for the job. Decide the order in which different steps for the job must be performed. Here the handbook will usually be of help. Part of your game plan should be in making sure you understand the function of the part(s) you're working on. You'll learn more by thinking this way, and you'll lessen the chance of making a mistake. As you go through the job, it's quite important to keep track of any parts you remove, and the order in which you remove them. There are plenty of ways to do this. You can keep a running log of the job and follow it backwards when you're replacing the parts you've removed. You can make diagrams as you work (especially helpful when working on the electrical system; note wire color, washer placement, etc.), which can then be used again. You might consider numbering paper cups and, as the parts come off, putting them in consecutive cups. The paper-cup idea is also a good way to keep track of different groups of nuts and bolts. You can tape parts to cardboard, or you can label them with tags and wire. These are only suggestions, and certainly there are other ways. You'll probably devise one of your own, which is fine. The point is, you can really save yourself a lot of grief by keeping track of what you're doing.

Because many of the procedures you are going to follow will depend on the particular bike you're working on, and since you are going to rely on the owner's handbook for them, what I'm going to do is give you tips that will be common to most bikes, and point out things that may not be in the handbook.

When the engine is involved, the two-stroke/four-stroke area makes a difference in almost all the jobs you'll be doing, so let's look first at things that don't pertain to the engine. Probably one of the most important elements in the way your bike handles is the tire air pressure. It is also one of the things that determines how long your tires last, and probably one of the easiest things to overlook. The handbook will give you recommended pressures, as well as alternate recommendations for extended high-speed riding and/or carrying passengers. The reason for the latter should be fairly obvious. The more weight on the bike, the more air is needed to keep the tire in a proper relationship with the road. The bit about extended high-speed has to do with the temperature of the air in the tire. Tire pressure readings should be taken when the tire is cold. The reason I mention it here is that the handbook may not mention it at all. Because the friction between the tire and the road produces heat, and heat causes air to expand, it stands to reason that the faster the tire rotates, the more heat will be produced, and the higher the pressure in the tire will rise. If you take long, fast trips, make it a point to check pressures at gas stops. If they're exceptionally high, let out a little, just a little, because if you slow down, tire temperature and pressure will go down, and you'll be motoring along on under-inflated rubber. Normally, you shouldn't have to check pressure more than once a week, but more often won't hurt and, naturally, if your bike starts handling strangely, don't ignore the possibility of a low tire. Try to check your pressure at the same place all the time, since there can be large differences in air-pump meters. Make it a place close to home so the tires won't get much of a chance to heat up. If you feel like owning another tool, there are plenty of reasonably accurate gauges available at reasonable prices.

On the subject of tires, another factor to consider is wheel balance and spoke adjustment. Both of these things can, and will, affect the way your bike rides, and the way your tires wear. Correcting either of these conditions had better be done by a mechanic the first few times. Watch, if you can, and ask questions. Even if you can't remedy these conditions yourself, you can learn to spot them. Make a practice of inspecting the tires visually. If you notice uneven wear, or a cupping condition, have somebody take a look at the bike. If you run your hand around the tread and feel more resistance going one way than in the other, it's probably due to heavy application of the brake. You can reverse the tire on the wheel to even out the wear, but it won't hurt to have someone look it over, just to make sure. Incidentally, some tires in the "off-road" group are only meant to go one way. Check for instructions or arrows on the tires' sidewalls. Make sure you use caps on the tire valves. They're there to keep dirt out. If, when you're inspecting, you find a nail or piece of metal, or anything that looks like it is going to cause a flat, don't pull it out unless you plan to fix the tire yourself. If you don't plan to, go straight to somebody who will. Fixing flats isn't a hard job, and you can get kits for patching tire tubes. Don't use anything but tire irons. Screwdrivers, the logical (?) substitute, will rip the tube every time.

Use a piece of chalk to mark the sidewall at the point where the valve stem comes through the rim, and the place where the nail was. Once you have the tire and the tube apart, lay the tube on the tire in the position it was in originally, and you will be able to find the hole in the tube. Marking the sidewall also helps you get the tire back on the wheel in the same relative position, which means you won't have affected the wheel balance much, if at all. Use a lubricant when you work the tire off or back on the wheel. A solution of soap and water works well. This will make the job easier and lessen the chances of damaging the tire casing. Once you have everything back together, put a drop of water in the valve stem. If you see bubbles, the valve is leaking and should be attended to. Keep a close watch on tire pressure for a couple of days afterwards.

If it's a rear tire, one of the things you'll have to disconnect (unless your bike has a quick-change hub, or a shaft drive) is the chain, an item which, sadly, is also in the "most-often-neglected" category. It seems strange that this is so, since chains are really simple to maintain. There are only two things you can do to a chain (three, if you count breaking them). The first, clean and lubricate. The second, adjust tension. If it's attended to on a regular (and frequent) basis, you can expect the chain to last for quite a long time. Be especially attentive to new chains. The first few hundred miles or so is the period when they will stretch most noticeably.

Drive chain is a series of rollers and plates which hold the rollers. There are bearing surfaces inside the rollers which must be clean and lubricated all the time if they are to perform their job efficiently. A snapped chain can wrap itself around all sorts of things, not the least of which might be your leg, and cause the back wheel to lock. (Hint: Don't remove your chain guard.) A broken chain can really do a job on engine cases, too, and that can mean an engine tear-down and new parts, neither of which are particularly cheap. So keep that chain in good shape.

As far as cleaning is concerned, the best way is to remove the chain and let it soak in a solvent. A word of caution here. Most thinners and cleaning solvents are flammable. They will burn quite willingly. Some can be poisonous if you breathe their fumes in an unventilated room. Make sure you use every precaution when working with these solutions. Use them outdoors. Don't use them near an open flame, or where there is any danger of an electrical spark coming in contact with the fumes. Store them in a cool, well-ventilated place. Make sure that containers are clearly marked, and where possible, use the approved alternate method for cleaning chain. Get somebody else to do it, at a garage or gas station. Many of these places have de-greasing equipment, and though they will charge you for the service, if you bring in the chain ready to be cleaned, the cost should be minimal.

Once the chain is clean, lubricate it right away. Although there are many ways to do this, the oldest method is still the best. Let the chain sit overnight in a pan of S.A.E. No. 20 motor oil. Number twenty is thin enough to penetrate and reach the bearing areas, and thick enough to provide good lubrication and cushioning effect. The soaking can be done indoors, since warmth will help the penetration, and the oil is not dangerous.

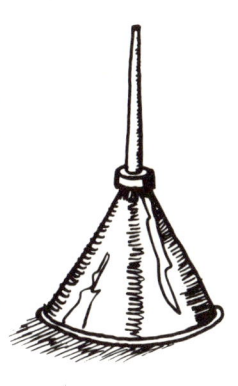

Before replacing the chain, wipe the excess oil off the side plates and rollers with a clean, soft cloth, and you're all set. Leave a film of oil on the chain to prevent the side plates from rusting. How often do you do this? You can't do it too often. The chain should be visually checked for rust where the side plates meet every time you ride. If you see it there, you can believe that the insides are dry as well and need some attention.

I said that there were other ways to lubricate chain, and there are. You don't have to go through the remove-and-soak business every time. As long as the chain is clean, leave it on the bike and use a hand oiling can full of No. 20. It should be noted, though, that the important thing is not to dump great quantities of oil on the chain, but rather, to get an adequate amount in where the bearings are. Drop the oil on the spot where the roller meets the side plate. Putting the bike on its center stand and rotating the rear wheel makes this fairly easy. There are commercial chain lubes, and many are quite good. Your dealer will probably recommend the one that he has found most successful. Most of the commercial lubes come in aerosol cans with spray tubes that let you get in close.

Pay special attention to the master link. It's the weakest one in the chain, and also the easiest to check. If it's dry, so are the rest. If your bike has a chain oiler that can be shut off, consider doing just that. Usually, all these systems accomplish is the over-oiling of everything but the chain.

The best time to lubricate a chain is when it's warm. This is true for a couple of reasons, and the only exception is when you're installing a new chain. Obviously, a new chain should be lubed before it's run at all, and the best way is the oil soak. Back to old chains. When the chain is warm, it has reached its loosest point. The clearances between the parts of the chain are at their largest, and it is much easier for the lubricant to penetrate.

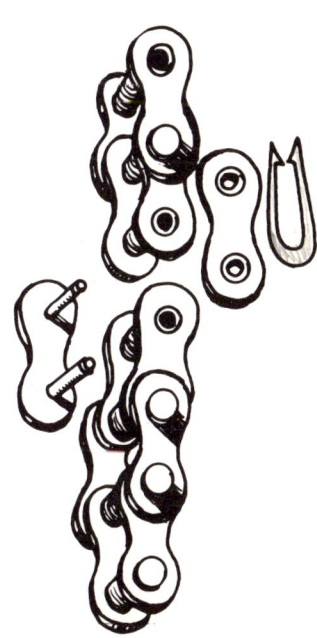

Proper adjustment of the chain is as important as proper lubrication, and should be checked as often. The chain should be warm for adjustment as well, so there is no problem in doing both jobs at the same time. There are two things to look at. The first is the amount of slack in the chain, and the second is the alignment of the back wheel. Put the bike on the center stand and loosen the adjustment on the back brake (you'll have to readjust it, anyway) so that the wheel can rotate freely. Rotate the wheel. Wiggle the chain up and down along its bottom run and see if there's one place where the chain is tightest. If there is, that's the position that the wheel should be in for the adjustment. Refer to the handbook for specifics on the amount of play there should be and finish the job by making sure that the wheel is square with the rest of the bike. Do this either by measuring the distance from the swing-arm bolt to the rear-axle nuts, or by sighting from behind the bike after making sure that the front wheel is pointing straight ahead. In fact, check it both ways. Now bolt everything back together and adjust the rear brake.

Probably the best rule of thumb for rear-brake adjustment is to tighten to the point at which the wheel starts to drag when you rotate it by hand, and then back off a little bit. The idea is to get maximum braking force with as little pedal movement as possible. Make sure to check your brake light. The brake-light switch works off the pedal or brake rod, and if the brake adjustment has changed enough, the switch may need adjusting, too.

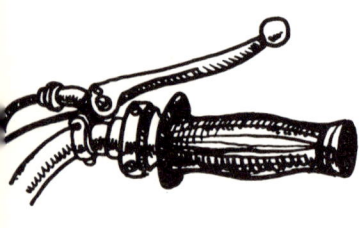

We did the back brake, let's do the front. It's time for me to say that no matter what anybody else says, you can and should use the front brake. It's vital to rapid, well-controlled stopping. It also must be adjusted properly. (You'll see that statement elsewhere in this book, but it's important, so I put it in wherever I can.) The idea is to get the front brake to work as hard as it can without locking up or skidding the front wheel. The way to go about this is a little tricky and it depends mostly on how the brake is adjusted before you begin adjusting it.

First, put the bike on the center stand. Chances are, this will raise the back wheel. Lift up the front and slide something under the front of the chassis to keep the front end in the air. Wooden or metal milk boxes are good, if you can get one. Rotate the front wheel. If it drags, the brake is too tight to start with; back off on the adjuster. Apply the brake lever and try to rotate the wheel in the direction of normal rotation. If you can do it, the brake is too loose. Somewhere between these two conditions is the right adjustment. You can approach it most safely by starting with the brake not tight enough. Generally, the brake adjuster will be on the handle, so it's not a very difficult job.

Sit on the bike and apply the brake as hard as you can. If the lever touches the handlebar, release it and adjust the lever so it doesn't quite touch the bar under hard pressure. Ride the bike. If the brake seems to pull the bike down well (don't forget to use the back brake, too), and you like the relationship between the lever and the bar, all well and good. If, however, you think you want the front brake to start working a little sooner, take up a little on the adjuster, but do it gradually.

What else is common to all bikes? They all have control cables, clutch, throttle, a front (and sometimes rear) brake, which have to be lubricated. The handbook tells you that, but it doesn't always spell out how to go about it. I use a method that works well. It takes a little time and it's not the neatest, but I don't worry about binding cables, and I don't replace them that often. In addition to keeping a light grease on the exposed portions of your cables, you might try this. The next time you're soaking your chain in good ol' No. 20, remove the cables you want to lubricate, coil them in upward spirals, and tie them with breadwrap twist-ties. Let them sit in the oil with the chain. Keep one end of the outer sleeve just above the oil so the air inside the cable can escape before you reinstall the cables, let them hang for awhile, and wipe the outside rather thoroughly. Otherwise, you'll wind up with a mess on the bike that sucks up dirt like a vacuum cleaner. This is even more important if the throttle cable ends inside the carburetor. If there is free oil in the cable, it winds up in the carburetor where it doesn't belong, so let the cable drain.

All bikes have carburetors. Most of the time nothing goes wrong with them. They are often misunderstood, in that they are the first things people try to blame when something does go wrong. But they don't get plugged if they get clean gas. They don't leak if they are kept tight. They don't choke unless they can't breathe. If you have a problem that says "carburetor," chances are it isn't. Since the function of a carburetor is the mixing of gasoline with air in the predetermined ratio, the one thing that is changeable in its operation is the ratio of mix, and the change is expressed in terms of how much gas is present in the mix.

A mixture with a large portion of gas is said to be "rich." One with a small portion is referred to as "lean." Pretty rough, right? In either case, there is a lot more air involved than there is gas. Probably somewhere around fifteen parts of air to one of gas. Without taking your carburetor apart, which you had better not do without more experience or help, there are only a couple of things that can be done. For that matter, they are really the only things that should have to be done, anyway, and they both deal with the way the bike runs at idle. They are (1) the idle mixture (ratio of gas/air), and (2) the idle speed (speed of the engine in rpm's). The two are not completely separate from each other, because the idle mixture will, to a certain extent, affect the idle speed. The handbook will probably give you settings for both, but it may not tell you to set the mixture first, and it may not tell you to make sure that the bike is thoroughly warmed up. It might not mention that if you do stop and go riding in a warm climate, you could stand a slightly higher idle speed. That type of driving tends to build up heat which can affect the smoothness of the idle and might cause you to stall while stopped at a light. Don't set your idle much higher, just a little.

Lastly, the handbook may not tell you to look for other causes of trouble before you attack the carburetor, though in the case of multiple carburetor setups (two or more), this is not always true, but I'll get to that in a minute. Think in terms of the simplest engine, one carburetor, one cylinder. The problem: rough idle. You can try adjusting the mixture. If it works, fine, but if it doesn't, don't run out and buy a new carburetor, and don't get discouraged. An orderly, step-by-step checklist will probably reveal the trouble quite quickly. Check the tightness of all hardware in the intake system. If the nuts that hold the carburetor to the manifold have vibrated loose, air will leak in through the joint and cause a lean condition. Check the air cleaner. A dirty one will restrict airflow and cause a rich condition. By the way, when you adjusted the mixture and cured the problem, you could have been covering up one of the conditions I just mentioned. If everything is tight, start the engine and gradually apply the choke. By doing this, you are making the mixture richer. If the idle smooths out, it means that the mixture was too lean. If all the nuts and bolts were tight, you could have a tiny piece of dirt in one of the internal passages of the carburetor which is restricting the flow of gas. It might go away, and it might not; but unless you're absolutely sure you can disassemble the thing, clean it, and put it back together correctly, don't. Let somebody else look at it. If, when you started making the mixture richer, the problem got worse immediately, it was too rich to start with. That could mean a bad float/needle valve and could be caused by a dirt particle preventing the needle from seating properly. Try tapping the carburetor body with the handle end of a screwdriver. It might free up. Tap—don't hit! If it turns out that dirt is the culprit, try to figure out how it got there in the first place and fix that, too.

With multiple carburetors, other ills are possible. The carburetors must be in balance with one another. Some bikes have balancing tubes running between the carburetors, but this doesn't mean the carburetors will take care of things by themselves. Treat them like individuals with individual cylinders. Follow handbook outlines. It's not that difficult a job to get them together. Also, make sure, if the handbook doesn't tell you, that the throttles are beginning to open at the same time. With individual cable setups the adjusters are up near the handlebar. With a linkage arrangement from carburetor to carburetor, the adjusters are somewhere on the linkage. Check (with the engine off) that the throttles are opening evenly, and reach full open at the same time.

There isn't anything tricky about changing oil, but there are some things that you can do to save yourself trouble. First and foremost, use an oil that is recommended by the manufacturer or the dealer. The oil that you drain out of your bike can tell you a lot. Whether it's gearbox oil, engine oil, or front fork oil, drain it into a clean container. Examine it. It will be dirty, no doubt, but it should be evenly dirty. You shouldn't see water or gasoline. Nothing but oil. Feel the oil. There shouldn't be any abrasiveness about it. If there is, it indicates metal wearing—not a good thing. If you're breaking in a new bike, some metal will be suspended in the oil, but it shouldn't be there long. Change oils when they're warm and let the oil drain for quite awhile. You'll be adding oil in quantities expressed in cubic centimeters. Ordinary baby bottles are graduated in cc's. Does that give you an idea? If there are oil filters that the handbook says to clean, clean them. They trap any particles that are floating around.

The two-cycle engine doesn't have adjustable valves. The four-cycle engine does, and you should be able to adjust them yourself. The handbook will give you correct settings and probably a procedure to follow. What you might have to decide on your own is whether the engine is supposed to be hot or cold. It makes quite a difference. If the recommended setting is somewhere between .004 and .008, it is probably a cold setting. Usually, when clearances in the teens (.015 to .018) are called for, the engine should be thoroughly warmed up.

The position that the camshaft is in is important, too. The valve you are setting should be in its "most-closed" position. In the case of the intake valve, this occurs when the piston is at the top of the compression stroke. The exhaust valve is freest at the beginning of the intake stroke. You are going to be rotating the engine by hand when you adjust valves. The handbook may not point out that this is much more easily done if you remove the spark plugs.

Before you put the plugs back in, take a look at them. Is the tip of the center electrode nice and flat? Is the outside electrode nice and flat? No? Well, you could probably use new plugs. Are there carbon or oil deposits around the electrodes? Yes? You could definitely use new plugs. When you buy the new ones, take the old ones with you. That way, you don't run the risk of getting the wrong plugs, and if you're clever about it, you can get somebody to look at the old ones and tell you how the engine is performing. Installing the new plugs is simple enough. The handbook will specify the correct gap. Your gap gauge should just slide in snugly. Start the plugs into the head by hand, and run them down with your fingers as far as you can. Then tighten with your plug wrench. Make them tight. But keep in mind that it's possible to strip the threads in the cylinder head by overtightening.

About the only tips I can give you on installing a set of points are these. Make absolutely sure that you know where all the wires and washers go before you take the old set out. Keep track of your parts. It's too easy to lose something that is small enough to blend in with Spaghetti-O's. Make sure you lubricate the point cam follower. Small tubes of grease are available specifically for that purpose. They're inexpensive, and one tube will last a long time.

There are lots of other jobs you can learn to do, and that you should learn to do. You can get a lot of satisfaction out of doing your own work, and you can save quite a bit of money. Just be sure to work at your own pace, and keep track of what you're doing. You'll be surprised how many new jobs are almost like the old ones.

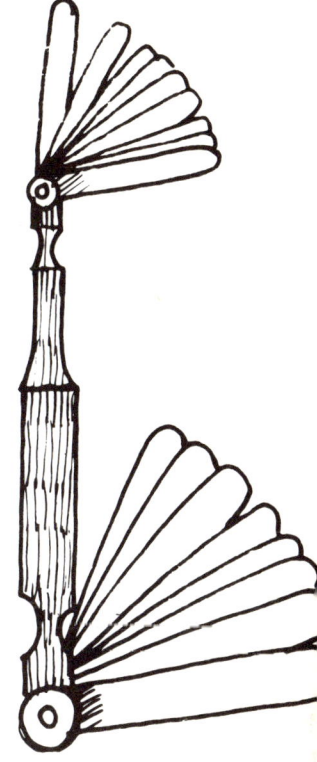

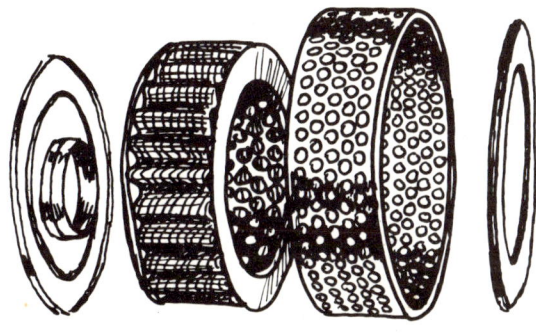

# THIS IS MY LEFT HAND

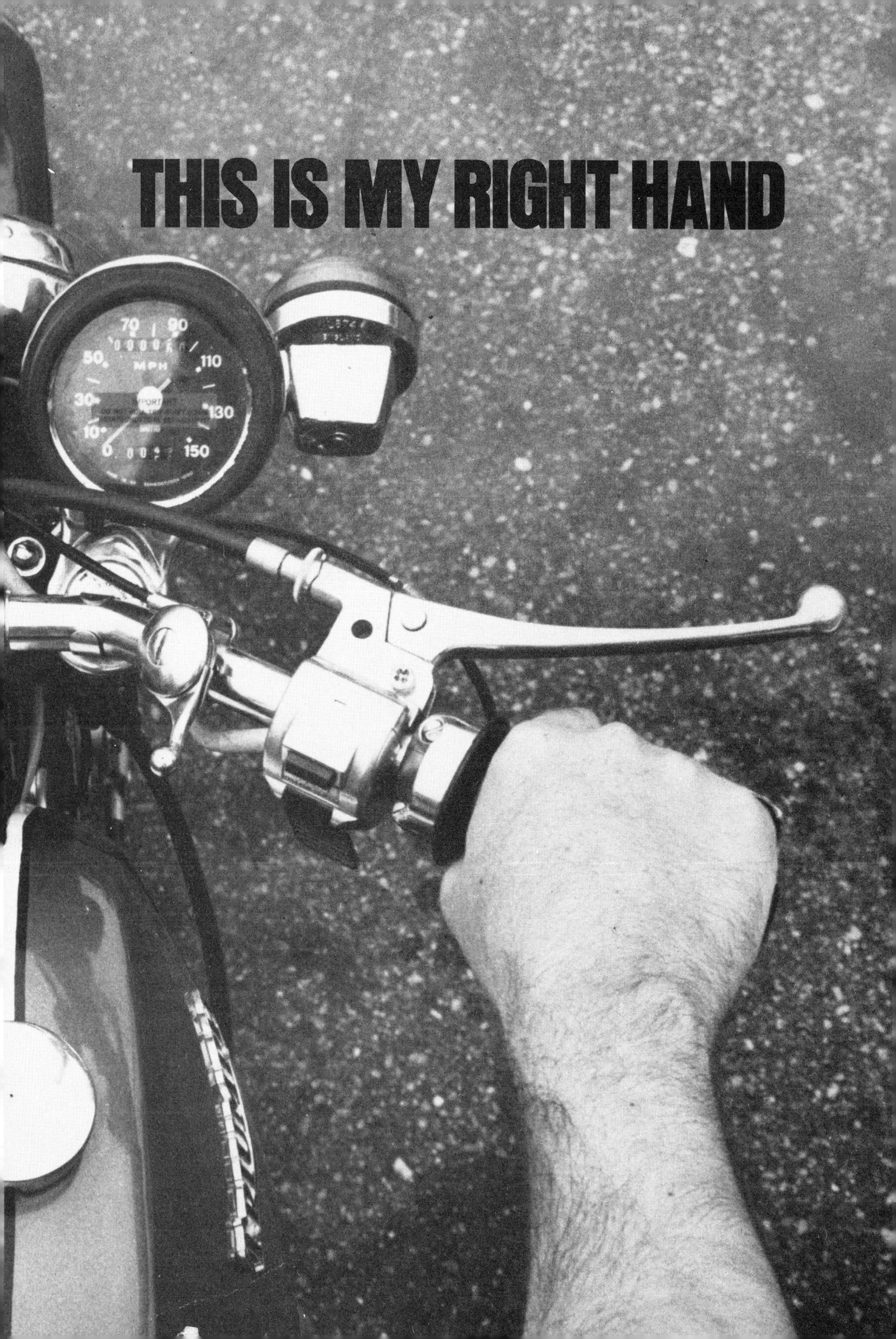
THIS IS MY RIGHT HAND
70
90
50
MPH
110
30
130
10
0
150

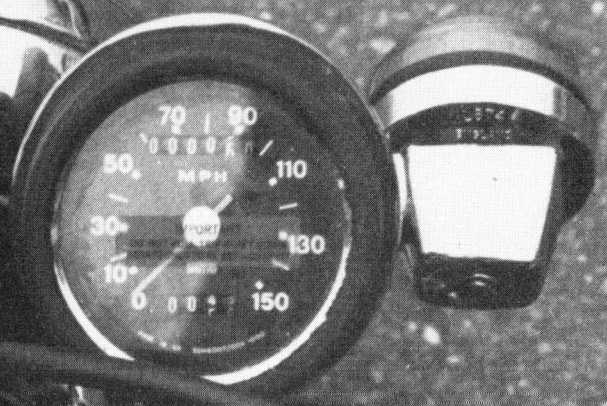

# AND THAT'S A MOTORCYCLE

The most important days you spend on a motorcycle will be the first days you spend on a motorcycle. Riders in their first year of riding have more accidents than those in any other group. The reasons for this vary. The fact that most first-year riders are also young people without much road experience is certainly one of the reasons. Of course, the accidents vary, too. Some are not very serious at all, while others couldn't be more so.

Those are the odds against you when you begin riding. So, finding a way to improve your chances of getting through with both you and your bike in one piece is a pretty good idea.

One of the best ways around is learning how to ride well and safely, though those two things are really one and the same. It's likely that you'll learn driving rules in a car, and that you'll get a driver's license based on the operation of a car. The rules apply to both automobiles and motorcycles, but they become more important when you ride a bike. In either case, following them accurately is the key to keeping out of trouble. This book will only talk about things that pertain to riding a motorcycle, but you should understand that those things are intended to be in addition to what you learn about using the highway in any vehicle.

Have you heard the term, "Defensive Driving"? It means operating your car or motorcycle with the attitude that you are ready to avoid

dangerous situations that other drivers create. An example might be making sure that as you approach a green traffic signal, the drivers who have the red signal are really stopped. If they aren't, *you* have to, or get clobbered. That's common sense. Checking to make sure is defensive driving.

Motorcycles are able to change direction quickly and safely. (It's because they are small and light, as compared to a car.) This is an advantage and helpful in riding defensively. The fact that they are smaller, however, makes defensive riding more necessary. People who are only partly paying attention to their driving may not see the motorcyclist. Defensive riding includes deciding that you're invisible, and that nobody knows you're there. You might consider riding with your lights on all the time. It helps.

Actual operation of a motorcycle is not difficult. If you are worried about balancing, don't be. If you can balance a bicycle, you can learn to balance a motorcycle. Bicycles and motorcycles do some of the balancing for you. Once moving, the wheels will hold themselves up. You can demonstrate this by rolling a coin across the floor. As long as it's moving, it won't fall over. The slower it goes, however, the less stable it becomes. Do I mean the faster you ride, the safer you are? No. I mean that while the bike is moving, it won't fall over on its own. When it is stopped, put your feet down.

You are probably going to learn to ride on somebody else's bike, which is good, because when you are learning there should be someone with you who already knows how to ride. Even if you're lucky enough to have a bike of your own, stay lucky and get someone to work with you. It almost (but not quite) goes without saying that the person who helps you should be a good driver/rider whom you have confidence in.

Find a place to learn. The best place is a large open piece of property that you have permission to use. Next best is large, open public property that you have permission to use (school parking lots, town equipment parking facilities, etc.). The worst place to learn is a street with traffic. Sure, that's where you're going to ride, but you have to learn the bike first.

Before you check the bike, check yourself and your clothing. Long pants and leather shoes or boots, yes. Canvas shoes, sandals, or the like, no. They offer little support and less protection. A long-sleeved shirt is a good idea, and, of course, if it's cold, some sort of jacket. Helmet, an absolute must. Eye protection, ditto. This kind of clothing is not reserved for learning. You should be properly dressed (protected) whenever you ride.

Put the bike on its stand and get familiar with the controls. The throttle is the right-hand grip. Turning it in toward you will open the throttle and cause the engine to run faster. Turning the throttle away from you will have the opposite effect. Also, there is a spring in, or on, the carburetor that draws the throttle closed when it isn't held open by the rider.

The left-hand grip does nothing. It used to, but not any more. The lever on the left handlebar is the clutch lever. It controls the connection between the engine and the transmission. With the clutch lever pulled in, the clutch is disengaged. With it out, the clutch is fully engaged. Pulling the control lever on the right operates the front brake.

Of the foot controls, one is the rear brake and the other is the gear selector. Either one can be on either side, since it is not standardized. Pushing down on the rear-brake pedal applies the brake, and pushing up or down on the gear selector engages a gear. The selector will remain in the middle of its travel when not in use.

There are either four or five speeds forward in the transmission (some have six), and a neutral. Gear-changing is accomplished by lifting or depressing the selector as far as it will go and releasing it. The selector will return to its middle position and be ready for the next gear change. The pattern is usually lifting for a higher gear, depressing for a lower gear. Neutral is usually between low and second gears.

The bike must have some method of starting. Some bikes have electric starters. The button will be on the right handle and is thumb-operated.

The other, and more common, method of starting is by kick lever, which the rider jumps down on. Get your friend to show you how to

This photo shows a clutch lever in the disengaged position. Once low gear is selected, the lever is gradually released and the bike begins to move. At the same time, the rider will open the throttle with his right hand by rolling the hand grip back.

Operation of the front brake. Increasing the pull on the lever increases the amount of braking. Proper use of the front brake is not hard to learn, but in spite of this many beginners, and some experienced riders, hesitate to use it. Learn — it's there for a good reason.

The bike in the photos, a Triumph, has its rear brake pedal mounted on the left side. Pushing down increases the amount of braking. Learn the limits of your rear wheel brake. They lock more easily than the front, because the weight of the bike and rider is transferred forward when stopping.

The Triumph gear selector is on the right. Pushing down engages low gear — lifting the pedal with the toe yields progressively higher gears. The pedal always returns to a central position after a gear selection, whether up-shifting or down-shifting.

start the bike a couple of times before you try it. With the engine running, sit on the bike and try the throttle. Notice how it controls the speed of the engine, paying particular attention to the fact that turning it away from you slows the engine.

At this point, get your friend to take you for a ride. Watch the way he coordinates the controls, both in starting off and stopping. Back in your learning area, go over the ride with him, and ask questions. Try to get to the point where you can explain to your friend how he operated the bike in a particular situation, and why he did it that way.

Start the bike. Tell your friend how you are going to engage low gear. You're telling him so you can be sure of what you're going to do, and so that he can correct you if you're about to make a mistake.

O.K., the engine is idling nicely, you have the clutch pulled in, and the gear selector has selected low gear with a little help from your foot. Gradually begin to release (engage) the clutch. As you do, gradually open (toward you) the throttle. The bike will move forward. Once you're rolling, pick up your feet and put them squarely on the pegs. Two reasons. One, it's the safest place, and two, that's where they have to be before you can stop, which is what you're going to do next.

Roll back on the throttle, pull in the clutch, and apply the brakes. Get into the habit of using both brakes. Gradual, even braking with both wheels is the safest, fastest way to stop. Staying in low gear, practice starts—the more, the better. Increase your speed a little each time.

Take a break and get your friend to go over changing gears with you. It isn't much different than starting from a stop. Let off on the gas, pull in the clutch, change the gear, let the clutch back out while you gradually bring the gas back on. It's a help if your practice place is large enough to permit large circles. You can keep going for awhile, shifting back and forth from low to second, starting and stopping, without having to turn around and come back the other way.

What you have done so far will probably have taken up the better part of an afternoon, which is fine, because at this point it's a good idea to spend some time going over what you've learned. It's also a good time for me to point out one thing. There is one rule that will be with you as long as you ride, which is: Never ride beyond your limit. Professional racers will say that the most dangerous aspect of racing is not so much the speed, it is the racer who rides "over the edge." It means that he's exceeding his ability to maintain control and/or pushing his bike beyond its capabilities. That makes him a danger to himself and the other racers. Think about it.

What you do the next time out pretty much depends on whether you have a driver's license. The object is to find a place to ride for awhile without stopping. That almost always comes out "country road," which, unless you own one, means a public ("Ya gotta have a license") road. But look around. You may be able to find someone with a private road who's willing to let you use it.

Let your friend do the driving on the way out. Again, pay attention to

*Kick starter operation—the lever travel is from nearly straight up to straight down. The pedal tucks out of the way when not in use.*

the way he operates the controls. When you get where you're going, talk about it. Practice a few starts and stops, and some low-gear, second-gear stuff to reacquaint yourself with the controls. By the way, even if you're on a private road, it doesn't mean that you're the only person using the road. If it's a public road, plan on other people using it.

Pick a stretch of reasonably straight road, and go. Don't do any more gear shifting, or go any faster than you feel comfortable about, and comfortable includes the traffic. If there is somebody coming the other way, move slightly to the outside of your side of the road, concentrate on your riding, and keep one eye on the approaching car. If a car is behind you, and you are going under the speed limit and/or the car wants to pass you, signal that you are pulling off the road, and do so. Most important: Don't make any harsh or rapid moves. They will upset both of you.

There will be a transition from pavement to dirt when you pull off. Be going slowly when you move onto the dirt, and brake sparingly. If the road is dirt to start with, look for it to get softer, and do the same thing.

Practice for quite a while. Notice how you're shifting the gears.

Smoothly? If not, why not? By now your friend is bored, so go back and talk to him. Discuss what you have been doing, and maybe have your lunch.

How much more you can learn this way depends on the progress you've made so far. If you're still unsure of yourself, insofar as actual operation of the bike is concerned, practice more. If you think you're ready, and your friend thinks you're ready, you're ready. Go ride. Ride wherever you think you can, but don't get "in over your head," and don't stop learning.

From here on, the thing that will make you a better rider is better riding. You don't have to go it alone. There are several ways of getting help in bettering your riding skills. Check the YMCA. Honda and the "Y" have organized a program for young riders. The program was started in Los Angeles in 1969, and its primary intent was to give kids who had been having trouble getting along in school or at home something to do. It has since become a national project with thirty-four states participating. If your YMCA is not active in the program, perhaps, if enough interest were shown, they might change their mind.

Talk to school people. Try to build enthusiasm among them and your friends who are interested in bikes, and you may be able to organize a club. Contact the motorcycle dealers in your area. They, or the manufacturers they represent, may have films or printed material on learning motorcycling, and they may be interested in working with your group. You'll never know until you try.

In 1972, the American Motorcycle Association developed the AMA Youth Division. It is a "totally separate [from the AMA proper] membership program designed for girls and boys 16 years of age and under, and directs its efforts toward fun and safety." Membership in the youth division is on a yearly basis at a cost of $8.00 per year. The $8.00 gives you a handbook on riding, a membership card which allows you to participate in AMA Youth Division events, a medical insurance plan that will cover you while you're participating in AMA youth events, and more.

Spend another 25¢. Write to PABATCO (Pacific Basin Trading Company). They're the distributor of Hodaka Motorcycles. Ask for a copy of their booklet, *Intelligent Motorcycling*. The booklet is a collection of articles on many different aspects of riding. The title of the book tells you what the articles are concerned with. The 25¢ covers book plus postage. It's worth more.

Although reading and talking about riding will never hurt you, it is not the key to becoming a good rider. It's up to you to exercise good judgment whenever you ride, to learn from the mistakes you make, and to encourage other people to follow your example. I said it before, but it's worth repeating. In the beginning, take it easy. Get somebody, a good rider, to work with you. Take pride in your riding. People will respect you for it, and maybe some day someone will ask you to teach *them*.

# MAKING SURE THE BIKE YOU BUY IS THE BIKE YOU WANT

Buying a bike is not difficult, but if you've never done it before, it can be a bit unsettling. A number of decisions must be made, and because there are as many bikes as there are to choose from, picking the bike that's right for you can turn into a real headache.

Begin by asking yourself what you want from the bike you buy. It's more important than deciding on one make over another. The best place to start is with size. There are big bikes, huge bikes, small bikes, and tiny bikes. How big are you?

Questions like, "Can I comfortably touch the ground?" are important to answer. If you can't, you are going to have a hard time starting and stopping. "Am I strong enough to lift it back up if it falls over?" and "How far can I push it if it breaks?" are also things to think about. On the other hand, don't buy a bike that is physically too small for you just because you are a beginner. You'll be tired of it before it's a month old.

A good way to get weight-and-size statistics, as well as other information, is to write to manufacturers. There is, in this book, a list of many of them and their addresses. Most will be happy to send you literature describing their products.

Generally, the bigger a bike is, the more powerful it is. Also, generally, the power that an engine develops is in proportion to its size, which is established by the volume of its cylinder. Volume means the

*This clutch lever is way out of adjustment. It should be drawn much closer to the cable sleeve. Either it is the wrong cable, it's the right cable and has stretched, or there is something wrong in the clutch mechanism. Cable adjustment may not cure the problem.*

amount of liquid or gas that it takes to fill the cylinder, under normal pressure, with the piston at the bottom of its travel. In the case of multi-cylinder engines, each cylinder's volume is added together to establish an overall size.

It is common practice of motorcycle manufacturers to incorporate numbers in the names of their bikes. Examples: Triumph Tiger 650; Suzuki T 250. These numbers indicate the size, or volume, of the engines. The unit of measurement is the cubic centimeter (cc).

How powerful the bike you buy should be will depend on a couple of things. One, how much riding experience you have, and two, what speeds you intend to travel at. Actually, those two things are almost one and the same. A new rider would be wise to restrict himself, in terms of fast riding, until he has a few miles in his pocket. It doesn't make sense to buy a bike that goes faster than you do. When you're learning to ride, a reasonably even-tempered bike can be a great help, since it is less likely to have you going over your head before you know what's happening. But don't undersell yourself by buying a bike that you will rapidly outgrow. If you plan to ride where speeds of 60 or 65 mph will be required, a bike that will only reach that speed is a safety hazard. You must have the ability to go faster. There can be situations where it is wiser to accelerate out of trouble than to try to stop to avoid it. You must be able to pass slow vehicles without creating a hazard by going too slowly yourself. Just remember that you don't have to go any faster than you want to, and in the beginning, you should probably go slower than that.

What are you going to use the bike for? Strictly road riding? Mostly off-road riding? A little of both? These are also things to consider. Knobby tires can get pretty uncomfortable on the highway after an hour or two of steady riding. If you do plan trips of any length, or don't like gas stations, the size of your bike's gas tank and the gas mileage you can expect to get are important to you. Do you plan to carry passengers? It takes power to do it safely.

Are there any laws in your state pertaining to rider age and the size of bike you can operate? Some states require by law that you be insured. Does your insurance company place any restrictions on what types of bike you may operate?

Once you have established the bike size you want, and what kind of riding you intend to do, you can begin to think about brands. There is a chart in this book that shows the different bikes that are available, and some information about them. Make a list of the bikes that fit your specifications and work from there.

Of the possible bikes you have picked, how many have dealerships within a reasonable distance from you? That's where you'll have to go for service or parts if you intend to do your own servicing. What is the reputation of the dealership? That's going to be a tough question to answer, but anything you can find out will be a help. Get more than one opinion. Get as many as you can, but make up your own mind.

What is the reputation of the bike itself? Here the opinion of the manufacturer or the dealer won't mean a great deal. The opinion of someone who has owned the bike in question will mean a lot. Again, try to get as many opinions as you can. A very good, and impartial, source of opinion is the motorcycle press—magazines written specifically for motorcyclists. One of the features of these magazines is "road testing." The magazine spends a great deal of time riding and testing individual bikes, and reports its findings. The people who do the testing are professional writers and long-time motorcyclists. Their opinions are worth a great deal. If you follow the sport, you will eventually find the two or three magazines you enjoy most. Subscribe to them. They will be well worth the investment.

Broken cylinder head fins affect cooling. How they got that way remains open for speculation. The bike may have fallen. The head may have been dropped from a work bench, or worse yet, the head may have been hammered into position on the cylinders.

O.K., you have it narrowed down to two or three choices. What's next? Ride them. See what each one is like. You might decide right away. If you don't, wait awhile and think about it. Most importantly, make up your own mind. Don't buy a bike because your friend has one just like it. Don't buy because the seller tells you it will be gone if you don't, unless you're absolutely sure it's the one particular bike you want. And don't buy a bargain bike, if it's one you've ruled out. Believe me, if money is a problem, you are better off waiting until you can afford the bike you want than you would be if you bought a bike you didn't want because you could afford it.

I've saved money for last because it is the final qualifier. It will determine, ultimately, what you buy, though not in the sense that it will make the difference between brands of bikes. You'll find that once you've decided what type of bike you want, brand for brand, there won't be much of a difference in the cost. How much money you have, or can get and are willing to spend, will probably determine whether you buy a new bike or a used one.

New bikes can break down, used ones can run forever, and the opposite is true. In either situation, there are things you can do to make sure you're going to get the best deal possible. If you're buying a new bike, you should have already done most of what you can. You know what you can expect the bike to do. You know the reputation of the dealership, and you have a pretty good idea what you're going to have to do to keep the bike going. If, however, your budget spells secondhand, there are other things to think about.

Repositioning of electrical components is common in customising. However, the wisdom of this location is questionable since the coils are now completely exposed to road damage and water, and the switches are not within easy reach while riding, which is not very safe.

You are going to have to figure out what condition the bike is in. Does it need work? How has it been cared for? You can approach these problems in different ways. Do you know the person that you're buying from? Don't buy a friend's bike because he's your friend. Buy it because it's the kind of bike you want, and it's in good shape. Does the bike appear to have been well maintained? A new coat of paint and shiny chrome are not always indications of proper maintenance. It's a small matter to clean a broken bike. Do I mean don't buy a bike if it's clean? No, I just mean don't buy a bike *because* it's clean. Look further. Lots of people take great pride in keeping their bikes clean. Probably they're

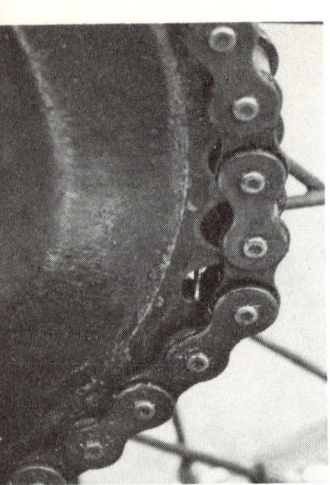

*A drive chain that can be pulled this far away from its sprocket has stretched considerably and should be replaced. Check also for sprocket wear.*

*This rear tire is well worn and should be replaced. The wear is reasonably even and indicates that the wheel and swing arm have been properly aligned. Wheel balance is good also.*

just as attentive to its servicing. It's up to you to make sure that that's the case.

Begin by visually inspecting the bike. Touch the engine. Is it hot? If it is, it could mean that the seller has been running it to make sure it will start. It could also mean that he just came back from an errand. Ask him. Check for broken parts. Why weren't they fixed?

Look for modifications, things that were not on the bike when it was new. Here it's helpful to know what the bike was supposed to look like originally. (That's called "doing your homework.") The owner can have done things to the bike that make it illegal. These things can be in the areas of lights (or the lack of them), mufflers (or the lack of them), fenders (or the lack of them). When you have the bike registered, you may have to have it inspected by the Motor Vehicle Department, which doesn't accept "I didn't know about that" as an excuse. Also, modifications of this sort may affect the safety of the bike. Take a good look. Know what is legal and what is not.

Check the control cables. Look for rust at the point where the inner cable connects to the lever or control, and look for cables that are frayed. You'll have to replace them. Why did the seller let them get that way? Check the chain. Is it rusty? Covered with dirt? Why hasn't it been serviced? Pull the chain from the back, where it goes around the sprocket. Does it come away from the sprocket? If it does, it has stretched quite a bit and could stand replacing.

How are the tires? Even wear is not surprising. Uneven, choppy wear means there is a problem somewhere else. Ask about it. Look for control adjusters that have no more adjustment left. It could mean that the things they control are worn out.

Look for oil leaks. Although they don't mean the bike is broken, they do indicate the fact that you'll have to contend with them. Some bikes leak oil, British four-strokes in particular, for the sheer joy of frustrating their owners. There isn't much you can do about it except replace the oil that leaks out. But if there's a puddle under the bike you're looking at, ask why it's there.

Sit on the bike. Try the controls. Do they operate smoothly? They should. Are you comfortable? You should be, both with your feet on the ground and on the foot pegs. If you're not comfortable sitting there, you won't be any more so riding.

Ask the seller to start the engine. (You'll have to get off.) He should know the starting procedure. You should, too (part of your homework). If it doesn't start on the first kick and the owner says, "It never starts on the first kick," it's probably true. If he has to say, "The thing takes awhile to get going," it's also probably true. You have to decide whether you're going to fix it, or kick as hard and as long as he does. If he says, "I can't understand it, it always starts on the first kick," forget it; it never does.

If you are insured, ask the seller to let you ride. If you are not, or he won't, ask him to take you for a ride. If he does let you ride, before you get too far, try the brakes. Make sure the bike will stop. If they chatter, or if they don't stop the bike quickly and smoothly, turn around. The last thing you want to do is get into trouble on someone else's bike. Assuming the brakes are O.K., ride awhile.

Try shifting gears. Pay attention to the operation of the clutch and the smoothness of the shifting mechanism. Think about the way the bike handles. Does it wobble? Is it traveling in a straight line when you are? Does it accelerate smoothly? Do you feel comfortable? Certainly, there will be a strangeness about a bike you haven't ridden before, but try to separate this from things that the bike should just not be doing. Again, do your homework.

Listen for strange noises. There will be some motor noise, but loud crunches and hammer-like banging are not in order. Ask about weird noises.

*Home made parts can be well made—this rear brake control rod, however, is not a very good example of the craft.*

If the owner won't let you ride, pay attention to the way he rides. If he won't take you for a ride, ask him why. "I don't feel like riding right now" or "The bike isn't ready" are not acceptable answers. If he wants to sell the bike, he should be willing to demonstrate it, and if the bike is worth buying in the first place, it should be ready to run. After the test ride, look again for oil puddles. They could have been wiped up.

If you have a friend who knows more about bikes than you do (and make sure), take him with you. If you know a mechanic who knows bikes, try to arrange with the seller to have the bike inspected.

Now that you've decided what size, what kind, and which bike to buy, and whether to buy it new or used, all that remains to be done is to decide how much to pay. If you're buying a new bike, all you can do is compare the prices of two or three dealers who are selling the same bike.

If you are buying a used bike, your insurance agent may be of some help. Tell him you are considering the purchase and you would like to know the cost of collision, fire, and theft coverage. Somewhere he will either ask you, or tell you, how much the bike is worth. If he asks you, tell him you don't know (which you don't), and he'll have to look it up in his rate book. Then you ask him how much it's worth. It will be a low figure, because it's the price the insurance company will pay if the bike is lost, burned, wrecked, or stolen.

Look in the newspaper. See if there are bikes for sale like the one you want. Consider that price too high. Figure the difference between the two figures and subtract something. That will be your bargaining figure, your starting bid.

At some point along all of this logical progression of thoughts, you are going to fall in love. There will be one bike that you absolutely must have, regardless of the sense of it. Go ahead, buy it. But no matter how many times the thing breaks down, no matter how often you tell yourself you must have been out of your mind when you bought it, no matter how broke the thing keeps you, remember that you loved it enough to want it in the first place, and that will help some.

*Harmony—between men, their machines, the earth, and all living things—nothing else is more important. It is not achieved easily, nor is it constant. It is the responsibility of all.*

# THE FOLKS WHO CARE

There are in the United States two major motorcycle organizations, both concerned with the growth and prosperity of the sport, but they approach their mutual goals from different positions. The Motorcycle Industry Council (MIC) is comprised of businessmen, motorcycle dealers and distributors, accessory manufacturers, members of the motorcycle press, and other people who work in motorcycle-related businesses. The American Motorcycle Association (AMA) is, with the exception of the people who work directly for the organization, made up of individual motorcyclists.

The MIC is the result of the restructuring in 1969 of another trade organization which had existed since 1914. The new MIC was formed to include a wider range of industry people with the intention of increasing its effectiveness, and to allow itself to work in more areas than had the previous group. At about the same time, the AMA took a look at motorcycling from its side of the fence and decided to do a little rearranging of its own. To that point, and since its establishment in 1924, the AMA had been principally regarded as a racing organization. It had devoted almost all of its efforts to competition-related activities, on both amateur and professional levels.

What the MIC and the AMA had realized was that the sport of motorcycling was growing quite rapidly, and if their organizations were to remain meaningful, they had to grow, too. Although each became aware of the need in different ways, and independently, the areas they chose to move into were much the same.

An increasing number of motorcyclists meant many things, not the least of which was the fact that government was now taking another look, too. Because many of the new riders were and are "off-road" enthusiasts, the subject of land management became, and remains, an important one. Sport and ecology groups who had previously enjoyed the wilderness on an almost exclusive basis had to face the problem that there was now another large group of people who wished to use the land. The motorcyclists' rights to the woods were, and still are, being fought about. The battleground is the Federal Bureau of Land Management and the Bureau of Outdoor Recreation. AMA and MIC involvement in the area of legislative representation on the part of the motorcyclist has grown remarkably. The AMA says that it intends to spend 25% of its effort in the area of legislation and land use in the coming year. The MIC's contribution will probably be similar.

Public relations is another area in which both organizations have become active. Here "public" means two things, riding public and non-riding public. "Relations" means getting along. It's a tricky, but necessary, place to be.

Because more and more new riders are also young riders, both the AMA and the MIC have developed educational programs. The MIC works with interested school systems, and the AMA has developed a Youth Division. The object, in either case, is to give beginning riders as complete a picture of motorcycling and its responsibilities as possible.

The work of these organizations is not as clear-cut or as limited as it may appear here. There are many other things that they do. Also, it's important to remember that they are not connected in any way except purpose—to further the sport of motorcycling. The work they do is vital and should be supported by every person in a position to do so. Motorcycling has come a long way in the last few years, but there is still a lot of work to do, and too few people to do it.

# GOOD GUYS/BAD GUYS

Motorcycling has not always enjoyed the best of reputations. At one point in the sport's history, the public's opinion of anybody who rode a bike was that he was an outright criminal or worse. There were a couple of reasons for this. While it was true that there were groups of riders who traveled in gangs, not always bothering to pay for things, and creating disturbances in the towns they rode through, their behavior on the whole was not a national topic of conversation. At one point, however, one gang actually captured a town. There was quite a bit of publicity which, needless to say, was all bad.

It was then that the country began suspecting the kid down the street of being not quite the all-around nice guy he had always seemed to be, even though he'd never before drawn any attention to himself. To make matters worse, the motion-picture industry began turning out "Outlaw Motorcycle" movies. At that point, if there was anybody left who had doubts about what cyclists were like, they didn't have them for long. All this was happening in the 1950's. Before that, cyclists were perhaps considered a little eccentric, but hardly the fearsome terror-spreaders they had now become. Although some riders and groups of riders realized that something had to be done about correcting the situation, and that it had to be done right away, the majority of riders accepted their fate and rode on.

Part of the problem lay in the bikes that were around to be ridden. They were large, and they were loud. One of the tricks of the time was to make them louder by removing what muffling they had. That made them seem even larger. British Twins, B.S.A.'s and Triumphs, and the American fire-breathers, Harley-Davidsons and Indians, were, by far, the favorite candidates for this treatment. Sure, there were lightweight bikes, but the selection was a small one, and there was little or no effort spent advertising their existence. As a result, people who might have ridden, had there been a bike they felt good about, or had they known more about riding in general, didn't ride, and the sport stayed small.

Then, in 1959, something happened that over the next few years completely changed the complexion of motorcycling. Honda arrived. A small, light, inexpensive, quiet, docile, generally lovable motorcycle was to change the nation's opinion and revitalize a tired industry. Honda's idea was a simple one. Make a product that would have a broad appeal, spend money advertising it, and in the advertising, do everything possible to promote the fact that the bike was nice.

The idea worked. It worked so well, in fact, that other Japanese companies were quick to follow Honda's example, and before long, Yamaha, Suzuki, and Kawasaki had joined the fray. Call it the Japanese invasion, call it the boom, call it whatever you like, it was a shot in the arm to the sport of motorcycling. As more and more people took to the road or to the woods, the "bad guy" image of the '50's began to disappear.

The "big bike" makers profited, too. They had a whole new group of potential buyers out there waiting to be convinced that they should "move up." All that remained to be done was reach them. Result: more advertising, and the quality of the bikes improved as well. It had to. One of the biggest attributes of the Japanese bikes was their reliability. They ran well and with a minimum of fuss.

The newcomers, however, had planned well. As soon as they attracted a following, they began producing larger bikes of their own. They figured that as long as a buyer was happy with one of their small bikes, he would come back to them when he wanted a bigger one, and they were right.

Since the early and mid-1960's, the sport has been growing, sometimes at alarming rates, sometimes not so, but always upward. That growth was not without growing pains. There was, and is, a constant need to keep the motorcycle image free of anything that would remind the general public (which really means "non-riding") of the old days. Now a new problem is facing the motorcyclist. Because his sport has reached the point that it has, the size that it has, it is once again being viewed with critical eyes.

The simple fact is that there are now so many of us, we are being noticed. The complaints are not new ones, but because there are more motorcyclists than ever before, the complaints are more frequent.

Noise. Soon motorcycles will have to comply with governmental standards which will specify the amount of noise a cycle will be permitted to produce. The system of measurement is a complicated one, and its explanation is not really necessary here. The legislation will probably be enacted on a state level, and will probably be argued about severely. That will bring about a bunch of laws that don't agree with each other, since what will be legal in one state won't be legal in another. Realizing the injustice of this, the federal government will come along and set standards for everybody, and whether those standards are fair or not, we'll have to live with them. It's not impossible to change federal law, but it's a lot harder than changing state law, and changing state law is hard enough.

The sad thing is that there is a need to regulate in the first place. If riders didn't make noise, there would be no need to force them not to, and noise is offensive. Take the mufflers off your bike and ride down a residential street. Change your clothes and go back on foot in a half hour. Ask people what they remember happening in the last half hour, and what they thought about it, and you'll see what I mean. Better, far better yet, imagine what they'll say. I don't want you to hurt the sport to prove my point, and believe me, you will. What's more, if you do try this experiment, you'll run the risk of getting a traffic ticket.

Off-road riders face another problem, that of land closure. There's good reason to protect the open land that remains in this country, as there is too little of it and it decreases at an alarming rate. It's not surprising that the people who use the land are concerned with its preservation. Those people include hunters, campers, hikers, horsemen, environmentalists in general, motorcyclists, and other people who simply enjoy the solitude of the wilderness. Public land is public land and everybody has a right to use it, but nobody has a right to misuse it.

The motorcyclist's position in this situation is a delicate one. He is faced with the problem of proving that he has as much right to the land as anybody else, and the arguments against him are strong ones. He makes noise. Noise disturbs wild life and people. His bike leaves tire tracks on the land, and that detracts from its beauty. Conclusion? He doesn't belong there. The fact that the rider can, and will, make his bike quiet, that campers can leave (and have left) garbage at their campsites, and that horses' hoofs do as much damage to the land as tires, carries too little weight with the governmental offices responsible for land management. Here the motorcyclist must work even harder to promote himself. He must demonstrate his willingness to protect the land he wishes to use, through sensible use of the land and communication with other groups of people who use it, as well as land management officials.

Even with the problems of today, the sport has come a long way, especially when you consider what it has had to overcome, but there is more to do, and the people who care about riding are the ones upon whose shoulders falls the responsibility of insuring that motorcycling continues to grow in the right direction. Take the responsibility seriously. It makes all the difference in the world.

At some point, probably the first point, you're going to have to convince somebody that motorcycling isn't the same thing as insanity and that all those "good" reasons why you shouldn't ride aren't really all that good. Realize right from the start that a person who has lived longer than you, and who has decided that motorcycle riding is dangerous, will not be easily convinced that he is wrong, or even that he should consider the possibility that he is wrong. Realize, too, that in some respects he is right. The truth is, motorcycling can be dangerous, but motorcycles are not.

Manufacturers spend much time and money designing bikes that will perform safely. Any unsafe condition that occurs after the bike is built is not the fault of the bike. So, you ask, why are there accidents? People, my friend, people is why. People who ask their bikes to do things they weren't designed to do have accidents. People who are not constantly watching what other drivers are doing have accidents. People who fail to maintain their bikes safely have accidents. And every one of them is unnecessary, and not the fault of the motorcycle.

... But there's no protection—you're out in the open.

Right, and there's also no chance of getting thrown through a windshield or trapped inside. Maybe automobile drivers should wear crash helmets and protective clothing the way most motorcyclists do.

... But if a driver isn't paying attention, he could run into you, and you'd be worse off on a bike than in a car.

Right again. That's why motorcyclists have to pay such close attention to what the car drivers are doing. It's why many riders keep their lights on during the day, and why they attach reflective material to their jackets and helmets.

... Is there any practical reason to ride a motorcycle? Aren't they just for fun?

Well, if that isn't reason enough, how about the fact that a motorcycle engine is about a tenth the size of an automobile engine, so it uses much less fuel and doesn't pollute as much air. Motorcycles are much smaller, too, and don't take up as much of what space is left.

... Are you trying to tell me that everybody should ride motorcycles because they're good for ecology?

No. All I'm saying is that motorcycles aren't as bad for the ecology as cars, and in one sense, that makes them more practical.

... Well, I don't think I'll ever be convinced that motorcycles are anything but dangerous, and that most of the people who ride them are anything but irresponsible, noisemaking bums.

If you feel that way, you might be guilty of making a decision before you know the facts. There are lots of motorcyclists working very hard to show the public that just the opposite is true. Maybe you owe it to yourself to find out a little more about motorcycling, before you make up your mind. I'll be happy to explain anything you want to know. Maybe you'd like to see a race.

... Yeah, maybe I would.

# THERE'S ONLY ONE NUMBE

**NO. 1**

You sit there. You sit there on a few thousand dollars worth of metal that's most of your life, and you wait for a flag. You think about all the other times you sat and waited, the other times you've lined up with your friends in all the other places. You think about the race. You think about the bike. The flag. The first turn, the win, and you wonder if the hours of practicing for it, the years of aching for it, the countless heartbreaks trying for it, square you with the people who still wonder why you're there. But you're a motorcycle racer. This is your job, and that's how it is. How it is every time you go to work. It's your job and it's your life. To keep on living, you have to figure you're paid up. Then, mechanically, the flag goes down and you're moving to the turn, the first turn. It's everything you've ever wanted, and everything you've ever dreaded. It's metal, noise, paint, and people. People with exactly the same reason for being there. To be first. To be the best. To be number one. Nobody settles for second.

Professional motorcycle racing is that intense. On the track there are no other thoughts but those of winning. To win a race a rider has to give 110%, and that includes all of his mind. At 140 miles per hour, he welds himself to the bike to cheat the wind. The two little patches of rubber where the tires touch the track are his connection. That's what he has to work with.

Of the many thousands of motorcyclists, there are probably no more than thirty men who are capable of being number one. They are special men. There is something in them that makes them need to compete on machines that would humble heroes.

The bikes are brutally aggressive, finely tuned in every respect. They bear little resemblance to the street bikes whose names they share. Frames, suspension, wheels, and tires, all are altered or replaced in the interest of speed. The bikes are set up for the track they are being raced on. Suspension and gearing is experimented with until, hopefully, just the right settings are found. The proof, however, is on the track.

There are different kinds of races. Road racing is only "road" in the sense that the tracks are paved. There are no intersections, no two-way streets, and no signs to tell you how fast you can go. Twisting up and down ribbons of asphalt that wind through third-gear sweepers and low-gear hairpin turns, open onto flat-out straightaways. The straights disappear into more hairpins or maybe into gradual turns that suddenly tighten. No two road-race tracks are alike. They have different lengths. Some are tight and curvy, while others seem like dragstrips with connecting corners. The one thing all tracks have in common is a start/finish line. It's just that some are farther away and harder to get to.

A road-racing motorcycle is like no other. Visually, the most outstanding thing about it is streamlining. A fiberglass fairing mounted on the front allows the bike to slip through the air with as little resistance as possible. The fairing incorporates a wind screen (which the rider will tuck in behind to get out of the breeze and further streamline

*Gary Nixon's form is faultless. He's an artist on the dirt and a composer on pavement—a smooth rider. Twice Grand National Champion, Gary's career and factory affiliations have taken him all over the world.*

*This is Evon DuHamel on his Kawasaki road racer. He's aggressive, calculating, Canadian — and very fast.*

the bike) and extends down, wrapping under and around the engine. Stubby "clip-on" handlebars point back and down. There is just enough bar to hold the lever and leave enough room for the rider's hand. The clip-ons, foot pegs that are mounted well rearward, and a very brief seat mounted well out over the rear wheel further helps the racer mold himself to the contours of the bike. Road racing is subtle. Often a small bike down on horsepower can come out on top. Getting through the turns is just as important as getting down the straights. On a tight track it's more important. A rider can build a lead in twisty sections of a course, and only give away part of it to the faster bikes on high-speed sections.

There's a flavor, a mood to racing. Road racing's mood is one of controlled, calculated effort. The urgency isn't obvious. It's there, but it's not what's seen because the style of road racing is smooth.

In flavor, dirt track is everything road racing isn't. It's no less precise, but it's blatant. Where road-race bikes are loud and piercing, dirt-track bikes are thunderous. The tracks themselves are dirt ovals. Two straights, two turns. The racers begin broadsliding before the end of each straight, continue through the corner, and out onto the next straight.

The tracks vary. Some are smooth and slippery, some are bumpy, and some have out-and-out potholes in them, but all of them are different. The texture of the dirt can change from race to race, and the riders must be constantly alert to these changes. What works in practice doesn't always work in the race.

Dirt-track bikes are not at home away from the track. Because the race is run to the left, and the bikes are leaned to precarious angles, exhaust pipes and foot controls get moved to the right side of the machine. Handlebars bend rearward for leverage. A recent rule change allows the use of a rear brake. Before that change, it was "no brakes" and riders relied on engine compression and broadsliding to "scrub off" the speed they built up on the straight.

Air cleaners, oil coolers, and megaphones jut out from the bike in seemingly peculiar positions. They're there because they have to be, and if something makes you faster, you don't worry if it looks a little strange.

In short-track racing, you win when everybody else loses. If you don't start first, you push people out of the way until you are first. Then you stay there. The races are "short" in terms of track length, and there is very little opportunity to pass. Strategy goes out the window. There's no such thing as holding back a little to conserve the bike. If you fall, there are a dozen riders ahead of you.

Rear brake only is the rule in short-track, too, and engine size is limited to no more than 250 cc's for two-stroke twins and 360 cc's for all others. Some short-track races are held on dirt and some on polished concrete, and often indoors in arenas or coliseums. The closeness of the racers and the crowd at an indoor race heightens the excitement.

T.T. (Tourist Trophy) racing is: a road race on dirt, usually including a jump, that requires dirt-track bikes with front brakes and even ground clearance on both sides. You can't get by on horsepower in T.T. racing. To be competitive, the bike must be absolutely willing to do exactly what the rider wants it to. It must handle precisely and with a minimum of coaxing, just like road racing. The bike also has to be able to handle the frame-shaking shudders of dirt. It has to work in any situation.

Motocross is a little different. The course is supposed to be tough. It's dirt, but smooth it's not, bumps, ruts, hills, jumps, drop-offs, waterholes (mud) included. True motocross bikes are light, powerful,

strong, and squirrelly. They have none of the niceties of street bikes. The engines are almost exclusively two strokes, and they're tuned for maximum power output. The power comes within a very small RPM range.

You win at motocross by doing two things. Getting as much of the engine's power on the ground as you can, and being strong enough to take the pounding that the track hands out.

A motocross event is run in heats, called motos. Each heat is of a specific length (30 to 45 minutes). The rider who's first at the end of the moto is awarded one point, and the second place man gets two points. Third gets three, fourth gets four, and so on. At the end of all the heats (two or three), the rider with the fewest points is the winner.

Riding as fast as you can for thirty minutes, over ground that would break a mountain goat, is exhausting. Doing it three times in one afternoon is almost beyond belief, but that's what it takes to win at motocross, and there are men who want to win.

An Enduro is an event that just about anybody with a woods bike can participate in. Enduros are run on an amateur basis, in that no money is paid to winners. There is no competition between riders in the sense that you would normally think, but rather, each rider is competing against a clock. The object is to maintain a predetermined average speed over a course that is filled with obstacles intended to delay you.

Each rider is assigned a specific time to leave the starting area. Since the mileage of the course is known, as are the speeds the riders are to maintain, there is also a specific time that each rider should reach the finish.

The courses are long. One hundred miles is not unusual. The event is broken up into loops, with rest stops in between, and some are run over a two-day period. Check points are positioned along the course. The riders should arrive at these points at a particular time, too, as mileage and speed are known.

A rider's time of arrival at checkpoints and at the finish determines his score. He starts the meet with 1,000 points. For each minute, early or late, from the time he should be at a given checkpoint, he is awarded penalty points, which get subtracted from his original 1,000. At the end of the event, the rider who has received the fewest penalty points is the winner.

The courses cover every imaginable type of terrain. Up and down rocky mountain slopes, through swamps and rivers, sand and thick woods, the Enduro rider follows his route card and the course markers that the sponsoring club has posted. The speeds he has to maintain aren't high, but a 15-mile-per-hour average is pretty hard to hold to if you spend 20 minutes unsticking yourself from two-foot mud.

Because the course often incorporates portions of public road as a means of moving the riders from one section to another, the bikes must be street legal. Lights, muffler, fenders, horn, etc. Apart from these required items, Enduro bikes are rather Spartan. They must be as

*Kawasaki powered, owner tailored, short track machinery.*

*This Harley Davidson TT bike is being flown by Scott Brelsford. Factory rides are hard to get. Scott got one when he was still a junior rider.*

*From front to back: a Penton, a Rickman, and a Bultaco, Sammy Miller Replica.*

*One of Yamaha's highly successful road racing trophy takers, and Mark's Bultaco.*

*One man, with one chance to qualify for the main event. Fractions of a second can separate the top riders. On the right is an Eagle motocross machine.*

*The view from the seat of a Yamaha road racer, and a Triumph Matisse. The Matisse is an early creation of the Rickman brothers.*

strong as tanks in order to survive the work they're put to, but they must be reasonably light, since there can be quite a bit of pushing involved in getting through the course.

I said before that almost anybody could participate. That is true, but not everybody finishes. By now, the reasons should be pretty obvious.

Bikes are competitive by nature, and so are riders. Because of this, motorcycle racing has been around as long as motorcycles, and it has existed, and still does, on every possible level. Today, American Motorcycle Association racing is the highest level, if for no other reason than that the AMA is the largest organized group of motorcyclists in the country. There are other reasons, though, and one of them is that the AMA has managed, through growth and endeavor, to standardize rules and regulations for competition. It means that, on a country-wide basis, riders can compete for points in a given classification of racing and be evenly judged with other people entering the same kinds of events.

The AMA breaks the country into districts, and the classifications into amateur and professional categories, with subdivisions thereof. Through the accumulation of points, a rider can work his way up through the ranks and, if he's good enough, become a professional.

The AMA assigns national numbers to the top 100 professional expert riders. There are, at this point, 200,000 AMA members. Naturally, not all of the 200,000 want to be professional racers, but even if 5% of them did, it would mean that 10,000 people would be competing against one another to be in the top 1% of their group.

Out of all this comes one man, one man who lives to race and races to be number one. He spends ten months out of the year traveling back and forth across the country. He races in AMA Nationals. That's the name the AMA gives to races that pay points toward the Grand National Championship.

Four kinds of racing are represented on the Grand National Circuit: Road Racing, Dirt Track, T.T. and Short Track. Each year there are a different number of national events. In 1972 there were twenty-three. National points are awarded on a finishing order basis. First gets the most. Then, depending on the amount of prize money the winner receives, the points are multiplied, but not by very much. Because road races pay more money, they are worth more in points. It evens out, though, because there are not as many road races as there are other races.

The National Champion is not the man who wins one or two or even three money races. The National Champion is the man who consistently finishes well in all the National events. He's good at his work, and his work is racing motorcycles, racing them on dirt, on asphalt, up hill and down. Sure, he can excel at one kind of racing. Most Grand National Champions do, but it's not that excellence that makes him number one. He's there because he's a professional—in every sense of the word.

# GLOSSARY

**Autolube:** Trade name of Yamaha oil-injection system.
**Berm:** Buildup of dirt around the outside of a turn.
**Big End:** Refers to crankshaft assembly. Bearings, crank, lower portion of the connecting rod.
**Bite:** Tire traction.
**Blown:** Supercharged.
**Blue Groove:** Hard, slick area in Dirt Track corners. *See Groove.*
**Blue Printing:** Method of extracting maximum performance from an engine. Precise mating of components, setting of clearances.
**Boonies:** Woods, isolated areas.
**Bottom End:** Lower range of engine's rpm's.
**Bottoming Out:** Occurs when forks or rear shocks reach their maximum compression.
**Bubble Shield:** Full face, clear plastic shield which bubbles out from the helmet.
**Contingency Money:** Prize money awarded by manufacturers to winners who use the manufacturer's product.
**Crossed Up:** Sliding at severe angles to the direction of travel.
**Cushion:** Loose dirt to the outside of a groove.
**Decible:** Unit of measurement of noise (db.).
**De-tune:** To decrease engine's power with the intention of making it more economical, or making it last longer.
**D.O.H.C.:** Dual Overhead Camshaft.
**Drafting:** A racing technique. Riding closely behind another rider to allow him to break the air in front of both riders.
**Endo:** Crashing. Going over the handlebars.
**E.T.:** Elapsed time. In drag racing, the time from start to finish.
**Expansion Chamber:** Two-stroke exhaust system. Gases in the chamber portion help to evacuate next gases from the cylinder.
**Fairing:** Streamlining device that can be fitted to the headlight/handlebar area, or to that area, and downward in front of the engine.
**Flat Head:** Refers to four-stroke engine with valves in the area of the cylinder block or barrel, rather than in the cylinder head.
**Flat Track:** A dirt track, but without any banking.
**Fork Brace:** Connects lower fork tubes to prevent wheel from flexing.

**Frontal Area:** Everything that presents itself to the wind when the bike is moving forward.
**Full Coverage Helmet:** Protects not only the head, but also the jaw, chin and mouth.
**Getting a Tow:** *See Drafting*.
**Getting Off:** To fall, crash.
**Groove:** Area of a race track which is the fastest path. Tracks can have more than one groove.

**Hack:** Sidecar.
**Hard Tail:** Bike without rear suspension.
**Hog (Hawg):** Slang expression for large Harley-Davidsons.
**Idiot Lights:** Indicators near other instruments which warn rider of things like low oil pressure or inadequate battery charging.
**I.S.D.T.:** International Six-day Trials.
**Jet:** Metering device in the carburetor which regulates gas flow.
**Knuckle Head:** Refers to a particular Harley-Davidson engine—the valve covers look like knuckles.
**L.S.R.:** Land Speed Record.
**Mid-range:** Usually refers to power output of an engine while operating in mid-rpm range.
**MX:** Motocross.
**Nacelle:** Headlight enclosure which also includes instruments. May extend down to cover upper forks.
**N.O.R.R.A.:** National Off-road Racing Association.
**O.H.C.:** Overhead camshaft. Camshaft is above cylinder and driven by chain or gears from crankshaft.
**Oil Injection:** Automatic method of mixing oil with gasoline, as used in two-stroke engines. Oil is pumped from a separate reservoir coordinated with throttle opening.
**One Lunger:** Single-cylinder engine.
**Overhead:** Refers to four-stroke engine with valves operating in cylinder head, as opposed to flat head.
**Pan Head:** Refers to a particular Harley-Davidson engine—the valve covers look like pans.
**Piston Port:** Basic method of fuel entry in two-stroke engine.
**Porting:** Improving gas flow by smoothing passages, polishing. Applies to both intake and exhaust.

**Port Timing:** Refers to two-stroke engines. Altering points of port opening and closing to improve power.

**Rear Sets:** Foot pegs and foot controls that have been moved rearward. Usually used with clip-on handlebars.

**Red Line:** Manufacturer's recommendation for maximum engine rpm.

**Reed Valve:** Used on two-stroke engines to prevent fresh mixture from blowing back into carburetor. Helps control crankcase loading. Improves performance.

**Rotary Valve:** Method of two-stroke engine fuel entry. Carburetor is mounted on crankcase. Flywheel is notched. Opens and closes over inlet port.

**Salt, The:** Usually refers to Bonneville Salt Flats.

**Side Hack:** Side car, or simply hack.

**Sissy Bar:** Accessory rising from behind seat which can be used by passenger as back support, and/or securing luggage.

**Slick:** Rear tire without tread grooves, used in drag racing to provide maximum traction.

**Sliders:** Lower movable portion of front forks.

**Stinger:** Final, narrow portion of an expansion chamber.

**Stroker:** Term applied to engines with long or increased piston stroke.

**Swing Arm:** Flexible rear section of chassis which holds rear wheel.

**The Ton:** One-hundred miles per hour.

**Thumper:** One-cylinder four-stroke engine.

**Tickle:** Refers to priming carburetors in preparation for starting engine.

**Top End:** Refers to the upper portion of engine's rpm range.

**Triple Clamp(s):** Connects fork tubes to chassis. There is an upper and lower triple clamp.

**V-twin:** Refers to two-cylinder engine with one forward and one rearward cylinder.

**Valve Float:** Occurs when engine's speed exceeds the valve spring's ability to completely close valves before next cycle.

**Wheelie:** Raising front wheel off the road under acceleration.

**Whoop-De-Doos:** A series of close bumps which cause a bike to bounce at speed.

**Works Machine, Works Bike:** Factory-built racer, maintained and raced by factory personnel.

# ADDRESS BOOK

American Motorcycle Association
P. O. Box 141
Westerville, Ohio 43081

(Attex)
ATV Manufacturing Company
1215 William Flynn Highway
Route 8
Glenshaw, Pennsylvania 15116

(Benelli)
Cosmopolitan Motors, Inc.
Jacksonville & Meadow Brook Roads
Hatboro, Pennsylvania 19040

(BMW)
Butler & Smith
Walnut Street & Hudson Avenue
Norwood, New Jersey 07648

Bultaco Services Incorporated
P. O. Box 101
Santa Clara, California 93512

Chaparral Industries
5995 N. Washington Street
Denver, Colorado 80216

Harley-Davidson Motor Company, Inc.
3700 West Juneau Avenue
Milwaukee, Wisconsin 53201

(Hodaka)
PABTCO
272 East Sherman Road
Athena, Oregon 97813

(Honda)
American Honda Motor Company, Inc.
P. O. Box 50-100
West Alondra Boulevard
Gardena, California 90247

Husqvarna Motorcorp East
1906 Broadway
Lorain, Ohio 44052

Indian Company
1535 West Rosencrans
Gardena, California 92049

Kawasaki Motor Corporation
1062 McGraw Avenue
Santa Ana, California 92705

(Maico)
Eastern Maico
Royal & Dude Streets
Reedsville, Pennsylvania 17804

Montesa Motorcycles
3657 Beverly Boulevard
Los Angeles, California 90004

Penton Motorcycles
1354 Colorado Avenue
Lorain, Ohio 44052

Rupp Industries, Inc.
Mansfield, Ohio 44903

Speedway Products, Inc.
160 East Longview
Mansfield, Ohio 44905

Steen's Incorporated
1635 West Valley Boulevard
Alhambra, California 91803

(Suzuki)
U.S. Suzuki Corporation
13767 Freeway Drive
Santa Fe Springs, California 90670

(Tarbo)
Chambers Enterprises
P. O. Box 20033
Long Beach, California 90801

(Tora)
Rockford Motors, Incorporated
1911 Harrison Avenue
Rockford, Illinois 61101

Triumph Motor Corporation
P. O. Box 6790
Baltimore, Maryland 21204

Yamaha International Corporation
P. O. Box 6000
Buena Park, California 90620